Contents

Introduction

"The last 25 years have seen the most dramatic reduction in extreme poverty the world has ever experienced. Yet dozens of countries have become poorer. More than a billion people still live on less than a dollar a day. Each year, 3 million people die from HIV/AIDS and 11 million children die before reaching their fifth birthday."

Kofi Annan, UN Secretary-General[1]

Across the world, 840 million people are chronically malnourished.[2] Nearly 11 million children die before the age of five each year.[3] Over 100 million (more than half of whom are girls) do not have access even to primary education.[4] This is not just an unfortunate reality of life. It is a human rights scandal of shocking proportions. There is therefore a responsibility to respond – a responsibility rooted not only in the demands of human decency, but also in legally binding international human rights obligations.

Gross economic and social inequality is an enduring reality in countries of all political colours, and all levels of development. In the midst of plenty, many are still unable to access even minimum levels of food, water, education, health care and housing. This is not only the result of a lack of resources, but also unwillingness, negligence and discrimination by governments and others. Many groups are specifically targeted because of who they are; those on the margins of society are often overlooked altogether.

The full realization of economic, social and cultural rights – including rights to food, housing, health, education and work – requires significant human, economic, technological and other resources. Yet limited resources are not the principal cause of widespread violations of economic, social and cultural rights, and cannot be used as an excuse to deny specific individuals and groups these rights. Ethnic minorities, indigenous peoples, women, members of opposition or religious groups, people living with HIV/AIDS or mental disabilities and many others risk deprivation as a result of discrimination and injustice.

Even wealthy and powerful governments have manifestly failed to meet their obligations to end hunger and preventable disease, and to eliminate illiteracy and homelessness in their own countries as well as internationally. Despite expressions of concern and statements of good intent, the international community has stood by while individual governments have disregarded the human rights of millions of people.

Denied farmland, seed grain and food aid in Zimbabwe

CK is 70 years old. She lives on a former large-scale commercial farm, where she has lived and worked all her life. When she retired, the farmer gave her a small piece of land for her food needs on the edge of the farm and a small stipend to support herself and her husband in their old age. Between 2000 and 2003 all of CK's children and their partners died of AIDS, leaving 12 grandchildren aged between three and 16 in her care. In 2003 the farm was acquired for resettlement and the farmer was forced to leave. The farm was subdivided and plots allocated to new farmers, including the land previously used by the farm workers. CK and the other farm workers could stay in their houses, but none was allocated a plot. CK now cannot grow food for her family. She was refused entry to the government's "food for work" programme or an allocation of maize from the government controlled Grain Marketing Board.

The government of Zimbabwe has failed to ensure food security during its "fast-tracked" land reform programme, which was ostensibly launched to address the massive inequality in land ownership. It redistributed large areas of previously productive land without ensuring that new occupiers had the seeds, fertilizer, tools or intention to grow crops. Together with the drought that afflicted southern Africa, this led to a huge reduction in available food. Food scarcity was exacerbated by the government's refusal of international humanitarian food relief and its use of hunger for political gain. Those considered opposition sympathizers faced significant obstacles in obtaining food through government operated distribution services. Among groups most affected by the food crisis were farm workers who continued to live on expropriated land and often had no security of tenure. Not only did the government overlook them, but they were also occasionally excluded from humanitarian assistance, as some international donors were apparently keen not to be seen to condone land occupation.[5]

Governments keen to encourage investment have often failed to ensure that big business respects its human rights responsibilities. They have exposed the population to danger through pollution, and to exploitation through denial of the right to a fair wage and decent working conditions. Acting alone or through international financial institutions, governments have often disregarded the rights of people elsewhere, supporting large-scale development projects which have resulted in widespread homelessness and violation of indigenous peoples' rights.

A pregnant woman has to wait for an ambulance to collect her at the Jubara checkpoint near Tulkarem, West Bank, 2004. Severe restrictions on the movement of Palestinians in the Israeli-Occupied Territories have had tragic consequences, with babies dying after their mothers were forced to give birth at checkpoints.

Violations of economic, social and cultural rights are not just a matter of inadequate resources; they are a matter of policy.[6]

Human rights are indivisible – all rights are of equal value and cannot be separated. Violations of economic, social and cultural rights – such as failure to protect the land rights of indigenous peoples, denying minorities' education rights and inequitable provision of health care – are often linked with civil and political rights violations in patterns of denial. No human right can be realized in isolation from other rights. Just as full enjoyment of the right to freedom of expression requires concerted efforts to realize the right to education, so the right to life requires steps to reduce infant mortality, epidemics and malnutrition.[7]

In adopting the Universal Declaration of Human Rights in 1948, the international community recognized that human beings can only achieve freedom from fear and want, as well as freedom of speech and belief, if conditions are created whereby all people can enjoy all human rights. Despite this commitment to the indivisibility of human rights, international attention has largely concentrated on certain violations of civil and political rights such as torture and ill-treatment, extrajudicial killings, "disappearances" and abuses of the right to fair trial. For more than 40 years, Amnesty International has played a leading role in putting these issues on the international agenda.

Since the end of the Cold War, however, the persistent denial of economic, social and cultural rights has raised increasing international concern. In all states, excluded or marginalized people still face barriers to realizing even minimum levels of their economic, social and cultural rights. Given this reality, campaigners are increasingly pointing to the imperative to recognize and combat such obstacles as human rights issues.

In recent years Amnesty International has broadened its mission in recognition that there are many more prisoners of poverty than prisoners of conscience, and that millions endure the torture of hunger and slow death from preventable disease. Given the interconnected nature of all human rights violations, engaging with economic, social and cultural rights has enabled Amnesty International to address complex human rights problems

"The arbitrary deprivation of life is not limited to the illicit act of homicide; it extends itself to the deprivation of the right to live with dignity. This outlook conceptualizes the right to life as belonging, at the same time, to the domain of civil and political rights, as well as economic, social and cultural rights, thus illustrating the interrelation and indivisibility of all human rights."

Antônio Cançado Trinidade, President of the Inter-American Court of Human Rights[8]

Denial of rights in the Israeli-Occupied Territories

In the Occupied Territories, restrictions on movement imposed by the Israeli army have frustrated the efforts of Palestinian farmers to grow and sell crops, and have denied Palestinians access to jobs and to health and education facilities. Blockades and other restrictions – including a 600 kilometre fence/wall under construction since 2002 – are imposed to keep Palestinians away from Israeli settlements and roads used by Israeli settlers. These settlements are illegal under international law and have deprived the local Palestinian population of water, land and other key resources.[9]

Women have been forced to give birth at checkpoints, sometimes with fatal consequences, because of their limited access to emergency medical care. Rula Ashtiya was forced to give birth on a dirt road by the Beit Furik checkpoint, in the West Bank, after Israeli soldiers refused her passage from her village to the nearby town of Nablus.

"We took a taxi and got off before the checkpoint because cars are not allowed near the checkpoint and we walked the rest of the way; I was in pain. At the checkpoint there were several soldiers; they were drinking coffee or tea and ignored us. Daoud approached to speak to the soldiers and one of them threatened him with his weapon... I was lying on the ground in the dust and I crawled behind a concrete block by the checkpoint to have some privacy and gave birth there, in the dust, like an animal. I held the baby in my arms and she moved a little but after a few minutes she died in my arms."[10]

in a more holistic and comprehensive manner. For example, Amnesty International's long-standing work on abuses in the Israeli-Occupied Territories has more recently addressed the impact of curfews and closures on the right to work and the right to health of the Palestinian population.

Campaigners around the world have mobilized since the mid-1980s in international networks to advance economic, social and cultural rights, sharing skills and experience learned over many years and in all parts of the world. Their efforts have led to improvements for certain individuals who have been targeted for abuse, recognition of the particular barriers faced by some groups within society, and greater awareness of the importance of these rights to the achievement of human dignity.

Economic, social and cultural rights are not mere aspirations, or goals to be achieved progressively over time. Under international law, states have immediate obligations, as well as longer-term duties. Regardless of their stage of development, states must take action to fulfil economic, social and cultural

> *"The dignity of an individual cannot and should not be divided into two spheres – that of civil and political and that of economic, social and cultural. The individual must be able to enjoy freedom from want as well as freedom from fear. The ultimate goal of ensuring respect for the dignity of an individual cannot be achieved without that person's enjoying all of his or her rights."*
>
> Circle of Rights: Economic, Social and Cultural Rights Activism: A Training Resource[11]

rights (including reviewing their laws and policies), and must refrain from violating these rights. States must ensure that there is no discrimination, whether direct or indirect, in the realization of these rights. Governments must also regulate the behaviour of private individuals, businesses and other non-state actors to ensure that they respect human rights.

As Amnesty International joins local communities and activists worldwide in campaigning for economic, social and cultural rights, this primer outlines some of the key features of these rights. It presents an overview of economic, social and cultural rights, outlines their scope and content, and gives examples of violations and what can be done to address them.

Amnesty International is convinced of the indivisibility of human rights, and the importance of campaigning to secure respect, protection and fulfilment of all human rights for all people. This primer highlights not only the obligations of governments within their own countries but also their international obligations, and the human rights responsibilities of a wider orbit of actors including international organizations and corporations.

As the international community has repeatedly recognized, all human rights are universal, indivisible, interdependent and interrelated.[12] Human dignity requires respect for all human rights of all people: there can be no higher priority than the right to live with dignity.

1. Reclaiming economic, social and cultural rights

Economic, social and cultural rights were marginalized for large parts of the 20th century, despite the recognition of the indivisibility of rights in the Universal Declaration of Human Rights. Human rights were not immune to the polarization of the world during the Cold War. On one side the achievement of economic, social and cultural rights was presented as requiring a political commitment to socialism. On the other, civil and political rights were portrayed as a luxury that could only be afforded once a certain level of economic development had been achieved.

Reclaiming economic, social and cultural rights as human rights has been achieved largely through the action of a large number of social activists around the world. Their messages gained greater resonance during the 1980s as global politics began to thaw and as concern grew at the collapse in social conditions and the prioritization of economic development over human dignity.

The origins of economic, social and cultural rights

Although economic, social and cultural rights are often described as "new" or "second generation" rights, they have in fact been recognized for centuries. Both the French and American national rights declarations in the late 18th century included concepts such as "the pursuit of happiness" and "égalité et fraternité" (equality and brotherhood), and the rights to form trade unions, to collective bargaining and to safe labour conditions. The first global human rights institution, the International Labour Organization (ILO), has protected workers' rights and a broader compass of human rights since 1919. Its Constitution recognizes that "universal and lasting peace can be established only if it is based upon social justice".[13]

The Universal Declaration of Human Rights[14] reiterated that "recognition of the inherent dignity and of the equal and inalienable rights of all members of the human family is the foundation of freedom, justice and peace in the world".[15] It went on to place a number of economic, social and cultural rights side by side with civil and political rights.

These include:

- the right to work, to just and fair conditions of employment, and to protection against unemployment
- the right to form and join trade unions
- the right to a standard of living adequate for health and well-being, including food, clothing, housing, medical care and social services, as well as security in the event of loss of livelihood, whether because of unemployment, sickness, disability, old age or any other reason
- the right to education, which shall be free and compulsory in its "elementary and fundamental" stages
- the right to participate in cultural and scientific life

From 1948 to 1966 the international community struggled to agree an international covenant on human rights to turn this declaration into binding international law. Ultimately, the intense ideological cleavages of the time led to the adoption of two separate covenants, one on economic, social and cultural rights and the other on civil and political rights. Differing approaches were taken in each. While states are required to "respect and ensure" civil and political rights, they are required only to "achieve progressively the full realization of" economic, social and cultural rights. Nevertheless, as shown below, both contain immediate obligations and obligations to be achieved progressively.

The International Covenant on Economic, Social and Cultural Rights, adopted in 1966, enshrines the economic, social and cultural rights contained in the Universal Declaration of Human Rights in more developed and legally binding form.[16] At the time of writing, 151 states had ratified the Covenant.[17]

The Covenant was, and remains, the most complete international standard on economic, social and cultural rights. However, international standards developed at around the same time in specialized agencies, such as the ILO and the UN Educational, Scientific and Cultural Organization (UNESCO), detailed specific human rights within their mandates. Also, since 1965 the international community has developed standards on rights relating to specific groups within society, for example, racial and ethnic groups, women, indigenous peoples and children. These standards contain relevant provisions on the application of economic, social and cultural rights to these groups. Regional human rights treaties in Africa, the Americas and Europe also provide protection for certain economic, social and cultural rights, as does a revised Arab Charter on Human Rights.

After the Cold War

Recognition and understanding of economic, social and cultural rights has strengthened in the last two decades in response to grassroots and broader civil society action. Social movements around the world increasingly mobilized from the mid-1980s against the stark social impact of rapid economic reform programmes, large-scale infrastructure projects, corruption and the unsustainable debt burden. Structural Adjustment Programmes promoted by international financial institutions, such as the World Bank, encouraged aid recipient countries to reduce social spending in sectors such as health and education and to devote a significant portion of their budget to managing their international debt. Countries instituted "cost-sharing" mechanisms that required people to pay for social services (often regardless of their ability to pay), resulting in collapses in primary school enrolment and obstructing access to health care. Claims opposing these policies were articulated in terms of social justice and, ultimately, human rights.

In the 1960s and 70s, certain civil and political rights violations quickly caught the imagination of politically conscious professionals – who were among those most affected. Similarly, the denial of economic, social and cultural rights required articulation by those most affected – by definition those with little access to political platforms – before being commonly understood as a human rights issue. During the late 1980s and the 1990s local and national activists were joined by international non-governmental organizations (NGOs) devoted to defending economic, social and cultural rights. An emerging movement culminated in global social forums and an international network where civil society organizations, committed to an array of social justice concerns, gathered to share experiences and build alliances.

Reclaiming rights as entitlements through public action gives legitimacy to calls for social justice. It stresses the accountability of a range of actors and duty-bearers, and has the power to mobilize global activism. Where the marginalized and dispossessed cannot look to their own government to respect, protect and fulfil these entitlements, duties of international cooperation and assistance demand action from those states that are in a position to assist.

The late 1980s also saw the establishment by the UN of an independent committee to monitor states' compliance with the International Covenant on Economic, Social and Cultural Rights, some 10 years later than the equivalent committee for the International Covenant on Civil and Political Rights. The Committee on Economic, Social and Cultural Rights analyses states' reports, makes recommendations for change, and issues General Comments on the scope of rights and obligations under the treaty.[18] General Comments aid international understanding of the nature of these rights and the obligations of states that have agreed to be bound by the Covenant.

Recognition of economic, social and cultural rights is not limited to grassroots campaigners, human rights defenders or UN bodies. Nobel Prize winning economist Amartya Sen, for example, defines famine in terms of a lack of entitlements. He considers that the right of access to food, and to the productive resources (such as land) that allow people to feed themselves, is essential to combating famine; food may be available, or even abundant, but often is still not accessible to all.[19]

Economic, social and cultural rights are now widely recognized as enforceable in the courts (justiciable) under both national and international law. In public interest litigation before the Supreme Court of India, the right to

life has been broadly interpreted to cover rights including those to education, health and freedom from the harmful effects of environmental degradation. Likewise, the Constitutional Court of South Africa has upheld economic, social and cultural rights included in the 1996 Constitution. It has developed an understanding of the state's duty to act "reasonably" to progressively ensure access to essential medicines and adequate housing, in particular through prioritizing the most vulnerable people. At the regional level, the African Commission on Human and Peoples'

A settlement of makeshift shelters houses a Roma community in the Patras area of Greece, January 2005. In June 2005, members of the Roma community in Patras were evicted and their houses torn down. In December 2004 the European Committee on Social Rights found that Greece had contravened the European Social Charter's commitment to uphold "the right of the family to social, legal and economic protection".The Committee stated that there were not enough good quality dwellings for settled Roma or stopping places for itinerant communities, and that Roma had been forcibly evicted from their homes in violation of the Charter.

Rights has found Nigeria in violation of several rights, including to health, housing and life, through failing to take sufficient measures to protect the Ogoni people from adverse impacts of oil exploration in the Niger Delta.[20] The European Court of Human Rights has also increasingly recognized the interdependence of human rights. Where the state failed to protect the population from the health impact of a polluting business, the Court found this to be in violation of their right to private, family life and the home.[21]

In addition, new mechanisms have been developed to allow victims of violations to enforce their economic, social and cultural rights. Both the Americas and Europe have adopted complaints procedures.[22] The UN Commission on Human Rights is also considering an Optional Protocol to the International Covenant on Economic, Social and Cultural Rights, which would allow an international remedy for victims who are denied remedies at the national level.[23] The Commission has also appointed a series of independent experts as Special Rapporteurs on the rights to education, adequate housing, adequate food and health, who report each year on the realization of these rights and carry out country visits.

Current challenges

Despite the advances, great challenges remain. Some influential states continue to be sceptical about the validity of individual claims to recognition and defence of these human rights. The USA, for example, has stated that,

> "at best, economic, social and cultural rights are goals that can only be achieved progressively, not guarantees. Therefore, while access to food, health services and quality education are the top of any list of development goals, to speak of them as rights turns the citizens of developing countries into objects of development rather than subjects in control of their own destiny."[24]

Consequently the USA has not ratified significant economic, social and cultural rights standards, and is opposed to developing international mechanisms to enforce these rights, including the Optional Protocol.

The view that economic, social and cultural rights are mere aspirations of development draws attention away from violations of those rights in both poor and wealthy states. A key challenge for human rights activists is to

Pursuing rights before regional bodies

Human rights organizations, including the Centre for Justice in International Law (CEJIL) and the International Centre for the Legal Protection of Human Rights (Interights), have intervened in economic, social and cultural rights cases before regional human rights mechanisms. They have submitted opinions known as *amicus curiae* (literally, friend of the court) briefs, and have represented victims of human rights violations.

CEJIL – along with the Movement of Dominico-Haitian Women Inc. (MUDAH) and the Human Rights Clinic of the University of California at Berkeley – is, at the time of writing, representing two young girls, Dilcia Yean and Violeta Bosico, before the Inter-American Court of Human Rights. The two girls have been denied nationality registration by the Dominican Republic, allegedly on the basis that they are of Haitian descent. Without registration, they will not be allowed to enrol in school, in violation of their right to education.[25]

reclaim the universality of rights by spotlighting and campaigning against abuses of economic, social and cultural rights around the world.

Yet the importance of integrating human rights into development cooperation is now recognized by UN agencies and various donor governments. The UN Development Programme (UNDP), in its Human Development Report, for example, has stated:

> "*A decent standard of living, adequate nutrition, health care and other social and economic achievements are not just development goals. They are human rights inherent in human freedom and dignity. But these rights do not mean an entitlement to a handout. They are claims to a set of social arrangements – norms, institutions, laws and enabling economic environment – that can best secure the enjoyment of these rights. It is thus the obligation of governments and others to implement policies to put these arrangements in place.*"[26]

However, implementation of the rights-based approach to development has been uneven at best.[27] Also, some UN agencies – including the World Bank Group and the International Monetary Fund – have not integrated this rights-based approach, even in areas where their work clearly has direct human rights implications.[28]

In addition to international development, the processes associated with economic globalization – the integration of the global economy, trade liberalization and the trend towards privatization of core public services – have brought new challenges to defending economic, social and cultural rights. Public service privatization is increasingly the norm, for example, and includes services essential for ensuring economic, social and cultural rights. Encouraging states to live up to international obligations to ensure that privatization does not negatively affect access to services such as water, health care and education is one of the priorities of campaigners for economic and social justice. Human rights activists bring an independent rights-based critique to such campaigns by highlighting the result of deregulation on the realization of human rights and compliance with the state's obligations under international law.

While trade liberalization may offer greater opportunities for access to previously closed markets for producers from developing countries, trade agreements often safeguard the interests of wealthy states, and their businesses, at the expense of people in developing countries. Human rights activists have increasingly voiced concern at the impact of international, regional and bilateral free trade agreements on the realization of human rights, particularly as regards access to essential medicines and respect for labour rights.[29]

The great advances in understanding and defence of economic, social and cultural rights, over the past two decades in particular, continue to be threatened by scepticism and denial. Self-interest is still prominent, and undermines international obligations to fulfil human rights. In response to global opportunities, as well as global threats, human rights and social justice activists have increasingly "globalized" in international partnerships to defend the rights of the marginalized.

Remaining scepticism about economic, social and cultural rights as full and legitimate human rights is based on the perception that their scope and content is unclear and that (unlike civil and political rights) it is often not possible to identify a clear violation, a violator and a remedy. The work done over the last two decades has to a great extent laid these misperceptions to rest.

2. Economic, social and cultural rights in focus

"There is no water-tight division between civil and political and economic, social and cultural rights".

European Court of Human Rights[30]

In many ways an arbitrary classification, the term "economic, social and cultural rights" covers a range of human rights, from rights to education, adequate housing, health, food and water, to the right to work and rights at work, as well as the cultural rights of minorities and indigenous peoples. The Universal Declaration of Human Rights did not divide rights into clusters of civil and political on the one hand and economic, social and cultural on the other, and for good reason. Some rights, including those of freedom of association and labour rights, are found in both international Covenants. Others, such as the right to education, include aspects that are traditionally perceived as civil rights and others as social rights. An outline of some of those rights generally classified as economic, social and cultural is presented here.

Cultural rights

Culture – the context of individuals' lives in their communities – can affect all aspects of human life from housing, food, the relationship with land and the natural environment, health care, religion, education and the arts. Related rights, such as the right to adequate food and to education, require that food and education policies be culturally appropriate.[31] Determining cultural appropriateness is complicated as "cultures" are never monolithic.

© Reuters

Members of the Xavante indigenous people confront a police line during a protest in Porto Seguro, Brazil, 22 April 2000. Thousands of individuals and several grassroots movements demonstrated against the celebrations of the 500th anniversary of the discovery of Brazil by Europeans. Hundreds of marchers were beaten by police officers who blocked them from going near the official parade.

Genuine opportunities for participation of minorities and indigenous peoples in particular, through respect for freedom of expression, freedom of association and the right to take part in political life, are thus a central element of respect for cultural rights.[32]

Cultural rights are protected in international standards in a diffuse way. The International Covenant on Economic, Social and Cultural Rights protects the right to participate in cultural life and to enjoy the benefits of science and culture. It outlines the duty of the state to preserve, develop and disseminate science and culture. More concrete provisions are found in international law relating to indigenous peoples (see Chapter 6) and in minority rights standards and those relating to the elimination of racial discrimination. Individuals and groups defending cultural rights internationally most often rely on the International Covenant on Civil and Political Rights (Article 27) which protects the rights of members of minorities, in community with others, to enjoy their own culture, to profess and practice their own religion, and to use their own language.[33]

Protecting the cultural rights of groups, communities and peoples must be balanced with the rights of individuals. The African Charter on Human and Peoples' Rights, which obliges members to promote and protect "morals and traditional values recognised by the community", has been applied to differentiate "positive" from "negative" cultural practices. Some, such as those that clearly subordinate women, may be in breach of other provisions of the African Charter. The Arab Charter on Human Rights requires that the measures adopted by state parties to achieve the right to the highest attainable standard of physical and mental health include "suppression of traditional practices which are harmful to the health of the individual".[34]

International standards to protect children's rights specifically oblige states to take steps to eliminate traditional or cultural practices harmful to children.[35]

The right to adequate food

There is more than enough food produced in the world to feed everyone, and yet hundreds of millions are chronically malnourished.[36] To comply with obligations related to the right to adequate food,[37] states must immediately tackle hunger and progressively ensure that "every man, woman and child, alone or in community with others, has physical and economic access at all times to adequate food or means for its procurement".[38]

Obligations to realize the right to food require the state to ensure:

- **Availability**: possibilities either for feeding oneself directly from productive land or other natural resources, or from well-functioning distribution, processing and market systems. This includes obligations of the state when acting internationally to ensure respect for the right to food in other countries, to protect that right, to facilitate access to food, and to provide the necessary aid when required.[39]

- **Accessibility**: both economic accessibility (through economic activity, appropriate subsidies or aid) and physical accessibility (in particular for vulnerable groups). The socially vulnerable or otherwise disadvantaged

Starvation as punishment in North Korea

"We were given corn-rice in small quantities. At times we got only salt soup with cabbage leaves. No meat was served. We were always hungry, and resorted to eating grass in spring. Three or four people died of malnutrition. When someone died, fellow prisoners delayed reporting his death to the authorities so that they could eat his allocated breakfast."

Kim spent four years in a penal labour colony for political prisoners at Yodok in the Democratic People's Republic of Korea (North Korea) after being repatriated from China and charged with treason. Hundreds of thousands of people died and many millions suffered chronic malnutrition in a famine in North Korea exacerbated by the actions of the authorities. The government prevented swift and equitable distribution of food aid, and prohibited the freedom of movement that would have allowed people to go in search of food.[40] Refugees forcibly returned to North Korea are routinely jailed and subjected to degrading treatment, including being seriously deprived of food.

may need attention through special programmes. They include victims of natural disasters and people living in disaster-prone areas.

- **Acceptability**: "The availability of food in a quantity and quality sufficient to satisfy the dietary needs of individuals, free from adverse substances, and acceptable within a given culture."[41]

As the African Commission on Human and Peoples' Rights found, in a case involving abuses surrounding oil exploration in Ogoniland, Nigeria:

> *"The African Charter and international law require and bind [states] to protect and improve existing food sources and to ensure access to adequate food for all... [Among other requirements] the right to food requires that the [government] should not destroy or contaminate food sources. It should not allow private parties to destroy or contaminate food sources, and prevent peoples' efforts to feed themselves."[42]*

One of the most basic obligations under the right to food is the duty on states not to starve those within their control, such as prisoners. As the UN Human Rights Committee has established, when the state arrests and detains individuals, it takes on direct responsibility to care for their lives, for example to provide adequate medical treatment, living conditions and food.[43] Human rights standards also speak to gender-specific aspects of the right to food, requiring states to meet the needs of women during pregnancy, confinement and after giving birth.[44]

The right to adequate housing

The Committee on Economic, Social and Cultural Rights has noted that more than one billion people worldwide lack adequate housing and that over 100 million are homeless.[45] "Without adequate housing, employment is difficult to secure and maintain, physical and mental health is threatened, education is impeded, violence is more easily perpetrated, privacy is impaired and relationships are strained."[46] Under the right to adequate housing, everyone should have a degree of security of tenure, protecting them from forced eviction, harassment and other threats. Services available should include safe drinking water, sanitation and energy. Housing should be accessible to all, including the poor, and priority should be given to the most vulnerable. According to international standards, states should take steps to ensure that

Forced evictions and housing rights in Angola

Between 2001 and 2003, an estimated 5,500 families were evicted from their homes in the informal urban settlements, or *musséques*, around Luanda, Angola's capital. Most of the *musséque* dwellers had sought safety in the city during the 27-year conflict, and built homes wherever they could find space. The government made no attempt to regulate house building or to provide amenities. From the late 1990s, Angola's oil boom created a demand for land. The *musséque* dwellers, who had no security of tenure, were vulnerable to developers.

In 2001 families in Boavista, an area near a cliff, were told that they were being evicted to save them from landslides. No attempt was made to secure the cliff or to hold meaningful consultations with residents. Instead, more than 4,000 families were moved to an area 40 kilometres away. There they lived in rotting tents for over two years while homes were built for them.

Residents of Soba Kapassa tried hard to obtain security of tenure, and carefully planned the roads and houses. Discussions with the authorities faltered, and in December 2002 residents were surprised by police and soldiers who surrounded the area while a demolition squad bulldozed houses. Altogether, 1,167 houses were destroyed. None of the Soba Kapassa residents was rehoused or otherwise compensated.

Over 470 houses were demolished in Benfica Commune between 2001 and 2003, again without meaningful consultations or prior notice. Most of those evicted were settled in new houses, some of which already had large lateral cracks in the walls, and in an area without schools or health facilities.

housing is located in safe areas, away from military sites, dangerous emissions or pollution; is near transport links and employment opportunities; and respects cultural rights.

Forced evictions, whereby people are removed involuntarily from their homes without legal protection or the assurance of alternative accommodation, are a gross violation of a range of human rights.[47] They often leave people at risk of damage to their health, unemployment and sexual abuse, and children unable to continue with their education. The Committee on Economic, Social and Cultural Rights has clarified that human rights law requires that people be ensured the greatest possible security of tenure, and that strict controls be placed on the circumstances in which evictions can take place.[48]

The right to education

The right to education encompasses the right to free and compulsory primary education, and increasing access to secondary, technical, vocational and higher education.[49] It cuts across the false divide between human rights, as it has civil, cultural, economic, political and social elements. Realizing people's right to education reduces their vulnerability to child labour, early marriage, discrimination and many other human rights abuses. It also increases their opportunities to realize other human rights, including the right to health and the right to participate in public affairs.[50]

States must ensure free and compulsory primary education as a matter of priority, and freedom of education (the right of parents to ensure education in conformity with their religious and philosophical convictions). To accord with human rights obligations, governments must ensure that education is adequately available; accessible (financially as well as physically); acceptable (it should respect cultural rights and the human rights of learners); and adaptable.

Minimum core elements of the right to education include prioritizing free and compulsory primary education for all children, and ensuring that educational content accords with human rights principles. This includes fostering diversity and understanding, rather than segregation and prejudice.

The right to health

The right to health is the right to the "highest attainable standard of physical and mental health" given the individual's genetic make-up and lifestyle

The right to education of minorities: Croatia

Within Europe, Romani communities face particularly widespread and grave violations of a compass of human rights, including the right to education.[51] Estimates suggest that up to a third of all Romani children in Croatia are completely excluded from the school system. Often Romani children who attend primary schools are in separate classes, where they are taught a reduced curriculum. The Croatian authorities seem willing to accommodate the demands of parents of non-Romani children that Roma be taught separately. Romani parents have pursued claims of segregation and discrimination through the Croatian court system and to the European Court of Human Rights. The lower Croatian courts rejected their complaints on the grounds that Romani children had inadequate knowledge of the Croatian language. A complaint that such segregation was unconstitutional, filed before the Croatian Constitutional Court in December 2002, was still pending in mid-2005.

In October 2003 the Croatian government adopted a National Program for Roma which, if implemented, may be a first step towards greater integration of members of Romani communities in Croatian schools and in Croatian society in general. The UN Committee on the Rights of the Child has pointed to the importance of ensuring this programme is properly resourced, in order to respect the right to education of Croatian Roma.[52]

choices, as well as the extent of scientific understanding and the maximum of resources available to the state. It encompasses freedoms (such as the right to control one's health and body) and entitlements (for example, to equality of access to health care), and consists of two basic components: healthy living conditions and health care.[53]

The Committee on Economic, Social and Cultural Rights has adopted a broad conception of the right to health, recognizing it as:

> *"an inclusive right extending not only to timely and appropriate health care but also to the underlying determinants of health, such as access to safe and potable water and adequate sanitation, an adequate supply of safe food, nutrition and housing, healthy occupational and environmental conditions, and access to health-related education and information, including on sexual and reproductive health. A further important aspect is the participation of the population in all health-related decision-making at the community, national and international levels."*[54]

To guide interpretation of the obligations under the right to health, the Committee outlined the following elements:[55]

- Adequate health care facilities, trained professionals and essential medicines must be **available**.
- Health facilities, goods, services and information on health must be physically and economically **accessible** to everyone without discrimination.
- Health facilities, goods, services and information must respect medical ethics, be culturally appropriate and sensitive to gender and life-cycle requirements in order to be **acceptable**.
- Health facilities, goods, services and information must also be scientifically and medically appropriate and of good **quality**. This requires, among other things, skilled medical personnel, scientifically approved and unexpired drugs and hospital equipment, safe and potable water, and adequate sanitation.[56]

Potential violations of the right to health include:

- deliberately withholding or intentionally misrepresenting information essential for the prevention or treatment of illness or disability
- promoting harmful substances
- failing to ban or discourage harmful cultural practices
- failing to control activities of corporations that have adverse impacts on health
- failing to adopt a detailed plan for realizing the minimum core obligations of the right to health [57]

The UN Special Rapporteur on the right of everyone to the highest attainable standard of physical and mental health (Special Rapporteur on the right to health) has enhanced understanding of the right to health, including sexual and reproductive health, and mental health. According to the Special Rapporteur's most recent annual report, while about 450 million people suffer from some form of mental disorder, over 90 per cent of countries have no mental health policy for children.[58] More than 40 per cent of countries have no mental health policy at all.[59] The report examines how people with mental health disorders are often denied equality in realizing numerous human rights, including rights to education, work, privacy, housing and liberty.

The Special Rapporteur has also explored the relationship between the right to health and the agenda of the World Trade Organization. Many free trade agreements restrict the production of generic medicines and greatly extend patent protections, and are likely to result in more expensive medicines that are less accessible to the poor without effective state subsidies.

The resulting conflict between states' human rights obligations to ensure that essential medicines are available to all, and the ratification of these trade agreements, has led to pressure for a public health exception to international patent protection rules. This exception is however frequently not replicated in regional or bilateral agreements.[60]

The right to water

In 2000 the World Health Organization estimated that 1.1 billion people did not have access to a water supply capable of providing them with the safe

Contamination and corporate accountability in India

The chemical plant explosion in Bhopal, India, in 1984 left thousands of people dead, many more ill, and pollution that continues to contaminate the air and fresh water supplies. "When you look at the water, you can see a thin layer of oil on it. All the pots in my house have become discoloured… We have to travel at least two kilometres to get clean water – to Chola Nakka. My health is so bad that it prevents me from carrying the water I need from there." Hasina Bi of Atal Ayub Nagar, a neighbourhood in Bhopal near the plant, has been drinking the water from the hand-pump near her house for 18 years.

Faujia, a 15-year-old girl, complained that "water is red here and it smells… like there is some medicine in it". Munni Bi said the water "is bitter… difficult to swallow." Their families live in Annu Nagar, an area in Bhopal, and the government freshwater tankers rarely, if ever, enter their neighbourhoods.[61]

The chemical plant was operated by Union Carbide India Limited, under the effective control of Union Carbide Chemical Corporation, a company based in the USA that has since been taken over by Dow Chemical Company. International human rights law places obligations on states, including India, to protect the population from human rights impacts of negligent company practice. Companies too have responsibilities to comply with human rights standards. Amnesty International is committed to working for corporate accountability for abuses of human rights, and has campaigned for the governments of India and of the USA (where Dow Chemical Company has its international headquarters) to comply with their international obligations to ensure that human rights are protected from corporate abuse.

drinking water necessary for a life with dignity.[62] Lack of safe water is a cause of serious illnesses such as diarrhoeal diseases, which kill over 2 million people every year (the vast majority children, mostly in developing countries).[63]

The right to water is increasingly recognized in international and regional human rights instruments, as well as in national constitutions.[64] Access to sufficient clean water and sanitation is essential to realize the right to health, to food and to secure livelihoods (for example, in food production). The right to water, like the right to food, has recently been interpreted to include securing sufficient availability, access (both physical and economic) and quality (free from harmful organisms or pollution).

As with other economic, social and cultural rights, priority should be given to the most vulnerable, that is to "those individuals and groups who have traditionally faced difficulties in exercising this right, including women, children, minority groups, indigenous peoples, refugees, asylum seekers, internally displaced persons, migrant workers, prisoners and detainees."[65]

The right to work and rights at work

Often derided as the right to a job and an obligation to ensure full employment, the right to work is perhaps the least understood of the economic, social and cultural rights discussed here.[66] Nevertheless, the right

Forced labour in Myanmar (Burma)

"Sometimes I had to work three times a week... Our NaSaKa [security forces] camp is large with 80 NaSaKa men, and 20 of them live in it with their families. There are a lot of houses in it and almost every day they need labour... The rich men can pay to avoid it and those connected to the authorities do not have to go. So the poor have to perform double duty. This is why I had to work up to three times a week. I also used to work as a sentry four times a month. So I did not have much time to work for my family. I could work for myself for about 15 days a month. I do not have any land and it was very difficult to survive."
A 50-year-old man from the Rohingya minority, Myanmar.[67]

Myanmar has long violated the prohibition of forced labour, among many other human rights violations. An ILO Commission of Inquiry found widespread and systematic abuses. Recent personal testimonies have confirmed reports that the army has deliberately targeted the Rohingya minority and that widespread corruption increases the disproportionate impact of forced labour on the poor.

to work entails at least the right to access to employment without discrimination, free choice of employment, and a supportive structure that aids access to employment, including appropriate vocational education.[68]

Rights at work, on the other hand, are more detailed. They include the right to fair wages, to equal pay for work of equal value, to safe and healthy working conditions, and to reasonable limitations on working hours, the prohibition of dismissal on the grounds of pregnancy, as well as equality of treatment in employment.

A particularly egregious violation of the right to free choice of work is forced labour – work exacted through the threat of some form of penalty, whether penal or the loss of rights or privileges.[69]

3. Obligations under international law

International standards on economic, social and cultural rights, although universally applicable, take into account the differing resources available to each state. They allow for the fact that full realization of these rights can only be achieved progressively over time, where sufficient human, technical and economic resources are available, including through international cooperation and assistance, such as development aid.

Duties to respect, protect and fulfil rights

Economic, social and cultural rights have often been seen as primarily "positive" obligations on states and derided as a "wish list".[70] In fact, being the "provider of last resort"[71] (stepping in where individuals and communities are otherwise unable to realize their rights) is only one element of the state's obligations.

State obligations to realize all human rights are of three types:

- to **respect**: not to interfere with the exercise of a right
- to **protect**: to ensure others do not interfere, primarily through effective regulation and remedies, and
- to **fulfil**: including to promote rights, facilitate access to rights, and provide for those unable to provide for themselves[72]

The obligation to **respect** human rights requires states to refrain from interfering directly or indirectly with people's enjoyment of human rights.[73] This is an immediate obligation. It includes respecting efforts people themselves make to realize their rights. Governments must not torture, unduly inhibit the right to strike, arbitrarily close private schools teaching in minority languages, or carry out forced evictions without due process of law or providing alternative accommodation, for example.

Under the obligation to **protect** human rights, states must prevent, investigate, punish and ensure redress for the harm caused by abuses of human rights by third parties – private individuals, commercial enterprises or other non-state actors. This is an immediate obligation. Governments must regulate and monitor, for instance, corporate use of private security firms, potentially hazardous industrial emissions, the treatment of workers by their employers, and the adequacy and appropriateness of services that the state delegates or privatizes, including private medical practices and private schools.[74]

States have an obligation to **fulfil** human rights by taking legislative, administrative, budgetary, judicial and other steps towards the full realization of human rights. This obligation should be realized progressively. This obligation includes duties to facilitate (increase access to resources and means of attaining rights) and provide (ensure that the whole population may realize their rights where they are unable to do so

Argentina: government ordered to produce vaccine

Within the duty to fulfil rights, states must prioritize their minimum core obligations. For the right to health, these include responding to epidemics. In 1998 a law student in Argentina, Mariela Cecilia Viceconte, together with the National Ombudsman, used the power of *amparo*, a form of class action to uphold constitutional rights, to demand that the state take more effective action to realize the right to health, and to respond to an epidemic of Argentine haemorrhagic fever threatening 3.5 million people.

The Federal Court of Appeals ordered that the state produce a vaccine, as the epidemic was unique to Argentina and the private sector saw the development of a vaccine as unprofitable. The court empowered the Ombudsman to monitor the implementation of its order, and held the Minister of Health personally accountable.[75]

In this case the court found that the state should take specific, concrete measures (developing a vaccine) to combat an epidemic that was unique to the country and where the private sector was unwilling to intervene.

themselves). The authorities must, for example, provide defendants with any necessary interpretation so that they can understand court proceedings, or introduce meaningful vocational training to ensure that students benefit from education. Above all, governments must give priority to meeting the minimum essential levels of each right, especially for the most vulnerable.

Immediate obligations and 'progressive realization'

The principal obligation on states under international human rights standards on economic, social and cultural rights is to achieve, progressively, the full realization of these rights according to the maximum of available resources ("progressive realization").[76] States have a duty to take deliberate, concrete and targeted steps, as "expeditiously and effectively as possible", towards fulfilling these rights.[77] Such measures might include adopting legislation or administrative, economic, financial, educational or social reforms, or establishing action programmes, appropriate oversight bodies or judicial procedures.[78]

In addition to the duty of progressive realization, states have various immediate obligations related to economic, social and cultural rights which are not dependent on available resources.[79]

The **duty to "take steps"** is an immediate obligation. The concept of progressive realization of rights does not justify government inaction on the grounds that a state has not reached a certain level of economic development. Conversely, taking steps to limit a right or taking retrogressive steps, for example by massively reducing investment in education or health services, can only be justified by an analysis of all the resources available to the state (including those available through international cooperation) and of the full range of obligations the state faces.[80]

To rely on circumstances beyond its control to justify rolling back the realization of rights, the state has to show that it could not reasonably have prevented the negative impact on the right. For example, the African Commission on Human and Peoples' Rights found that Zaire (as the Democratic Republic of the Congo was then named) had violated the right to education when secondary schools and universities were closed for two years during a period of armed conflict.[81]

Another immediate obligation is the state's **duty to prioritize "minimum core obligations"**, minimum essential levels of each of the rights. Under the right to education, for example, core obligations include the right to free and compulsory primary education, and ensuring that children are not taught in a racist, homophobic or otherwise discriminatory way. Under the right to health, states must ensure access to

The Aliev family, who were told that their home would be demolished as it had been built without official permission, Krasnodar Terroritory, southwest Russian Federation, May 2002. The largely Muslim Meskhetian community, although citizens of the former Soviet Union living in the Russian Federation when the 1992 Citizenship Law came into force, was denied citizenship. Without recognition as citizens, the family were unable to officially register their house or land. The state's duty to respect the right to adequate housing includes not evicting people without due process, warning or alternative accommodation.

essential medicines, emergency care and pre- and post-natal care. To justify
a failure to fulfil core obligations, states must show that they have done all
within their power.

> *"A State party in which any significant number of individuals is
> deprived of essential foodstuffs, of essential primary health care,
> of basic shelter and housing, or of the most basic forms of
> education is,* prima facie, *failing to discharge its obligations under
> the Covenant."*[82]

The **duty not to discriminate** is also an immediate obligation. The
adoption of laws, policies or practices that have a direct or indirect
discriminatory impact on the ability of people to realize their rights amounts
to a human rights violation.

The **duty to prioritize the most vulnerable** is also an immediate
obligation. The state should actively reach out to marginalized and excluded
people, who face the greatest barriers in realizing their rights, and they should
be given "first call"[83] when allocating resources.

> *"Even in times of severe resources constraints...vulnerable
> members of society can and indeed must be protected by the
> adoption of relatively low-cost targeted programs."*[84]

Obligations beyond borders

> *"In addition to the separate responsibilities each state bears towards
> its own society, states are, collectively, the custodians of our
> common life on this planet – a life the citizens of all countries
> share."*
> Kofi Annan, UN Secretary-General[85]

With the growing influence of transnational corporations, the globalization of
labour and finance, and increasing moves to link development cooperation
with human rights, the international dimensions of human rights obligations
are more important than ever.

In view of the glaring economic power imbalances between countries of
the north and south, international cooperation and assistance is crucial to

realizing economic, social and cultural rights of all people. However international cooperation can have either positive or negative effects. It is not always based on human rights principles, such as non-discrimination or prioritizing minimum essential levels of each right. It does not always focus on those who are excluded, marginalized or the most vulnerable.

States' obligations to respect, protect and fulfil economic, social and cultural rights are not limited to their own jurisdictions and territories under their effective control, but extend to actions beyond their borders.[86] When state action in another country directly undermines the ability of that country's population to realize their rights (failure to respect rights abroad), or where failure to regulate domestic actors results in human rights abuse abroad (failure to protect rights abroad), states should be held to account.

Despite increasing attention to issues of development cooperation, there is little awareness that international assistance is a human rights obligation, and not merely a question of charity or enlightened self-interest.

All UN member states have pledged to take joint and separate action to achieve universal respect for, and observance of, human rights for all without distinction.[87] International standards oblige states to take steps, individually

Nigeria: forced evictions the price of development?

A World Bank-funded project to improve drainage and sanitation in impoverished districts of Lagos, Nigeria, was halted after a local human rights group complained that thousands of people had been forcibly evicted from their homes. The Social and Economic Rights Action Center (SERAC) in 1998 petitioned the World Bank's Inspection Panel, a body created by the Bank to provide an independent forum to analyse complaints that projects supported by the World Bank have not followed the Bank's own operating policies, causing harm.[88]

A member of the Inspection Panel visited the affected site, talked with the local communities, World Bank staff, SERAC, officials and contractors. The Panel concluded that some of the affected communities had not received adequate notice of eviction or any compensation for their loss, in contravention of the Bank's own operating policies.[89] The Panel sought to use its good offices to ensure that the failings were rectified.[90] The project was reported to have been halted, pending compensation and resettlement of those affected.[91] Nevertheless, SERAC continued to report mass evictions of residents who were part of these communities, even as litigation on their behalf continued.[92]

and through international assistance and cooperation, according to the maximum of available resources, towards the full realization of economic, social and cultural rights.[93]

International cooperation must at all times be based on consent.[94] However, states are required to seek international assistance where they cannot meet their minimum core obligations.[95] In the spirit of this international pledge, countries that are genuinely committed to realizing minimum essential levels of rights, and have taken all reasonable measures to do so, should be provided additional resources from those states "in a position to provide assistance".[96]

Confronting human rights failures of development cooperation has, until now, been achieved primarily through analysing whether development assistance policies are rights-based in practice.[97] Recently, however, the UN Committee on Economic, Social and Cultural Rights has begun to analyse states' development cooperation policies, and even to call for greater resources to be made available through international cooperation.[98]

The current global focus on achieving the UN Millennium Development Goals represents a tremendous opportunity for civil society to capitalize on

Millennium Development Goals

All UN member states have pledged to achieve by 2015 the UN Millennium Development Goals, eight goals that represent an unprecedented international opportunity to ameliorate social conditions in developing countries:[99]

- halving extreme poverty and hunger
- achieving universal primary education
- promoting gender equality and empowering women
- reducing the mortality rate of children under five by two-thirds
- reducing the rate of women dying in childbirth by three-quarters
- reversing the spread of HIV/AIDS, malaria and other major diseases
- ensuring environmental sustainability, including by halving the proportion of people without access to safe drinking water
- developing a global partnership for development, with targets for aid, trade and debt relief

the attention the Goals could potentially give to economic, social and cultural rights over the next 10 years. However, some of the Goals appear to set levels of expected achievement lower than those that states are required to meet under international law. The Goal of halving hunger, if met, would hugely increase life expectancy, health and human dignity. Yet the 151 states that have ratified the International Covenant on Economic, Social and Cultural Rights are already required to ensure, at the very least, that everyone is free from hunger. Such legal obligations are rarely integrated in the consideration of the achievement of the Goals. In addition, the Goals reflect only partially the spectrum of economic, social and cultural rights issues that states are obliged to address. Also, they exclude civil and political rights such as freedom of expression and association, despite global acceptance that rights are rarely realized where individuals are denied the freedom to mobilize in defence of their rights.

Moreover, concentrating on abstract and average targets such as this must not allow patterns of injustice to go unchallenged. Marginalized groups, including displaced people, indigenous peoples, migrants, minorities, refugees and women, are often overlooked. Progress towards these Goals needs to be analysed to see whether it is consistent with legal obligations to ensure non-discrimination. For example, increased numbers of children in school should not cloak the reality of an essentially unilingual, monocultural or segregated school system. The collection of data to identify progress towards each Goal among marginalized groups and the integration of human rights into monitoring the Goals are crucial to ensuring that the Goals contribute to the full realization of human rights.

4. Identifying violations of economic, social and cultural rights

> *"A violation of economic, social and cultural rights occurs when a State pursues, by action or omission, a policy or practice which deliberately contravenes or ignores obligations of the Covenant."*
> Maastricht Guidelines on Violations of Economic, Social and Cultural Rights[100]

Much scepticism about economic, social and cultural rights is the result of feelings of helplessness or resignation in the face of overwhelming statistics on deprivation.[101] Can all 840 million people who do not have access to nutritionally adequate food be victims of human rights violations?

Initial resistance to the recognition of economic, social and cultural rights as human rights stemmed in part from the perceived difficulty of monitoring and assessing the "progressive realization" of these rights. This would require the collection of reliable data, appropriately disaggregated according to each of the prohibited grounds of discrimination, as well as effective indicators to identify progress (or lack of progress) towards full realization. Attempts to identify appropriate indicators have advanced slowly.[102]

However, faster progress has been made in developing a "violations based approach", identifying states' failures to meet immediate obligations or minimum core obligations.[103] Many organizations working on economic, social and cultural rights have adopted this approach, applying many of the techniques developed for monitoring civil and political rights violations.

What constitutes a violation?

A framework for assessing possible violations of economic, social and cultural rights has been developed through international expert seminars in 1986 and 1996, and confirmed by subsequent case law.[104] These include situations where a state:

- fails to respect or protect a right or to remove obstacles to its immediate fulfilment (for example, through forced eviction or failing to adequately regulate private service providers)
- employs policies or practices with the intent or effect of discriminating against certain groups or individuals on impermissible grounds (for example, where health care professionals speak only official languages, not minority languages)
- fails to realize without delay a minimum core obligation (for example, failing to prioritize free and compulsory primary education)
- fails to take prompt, concrete and targeted steps towards the full realization of a right (for example, failing to plan for essential medicines to be affordable and available to all)
- fails to adequately prioritize the realization of minimum essential levels of each right, particularly for marginalized people, the excluded and the vulnerable (for example, investing heavily in improving the environment of wealthier districts and little on ensuring the safety of shanty towns)
- places a limitation, not recognized in international law, on the exercise of a right[105] (for example, restricting the right to security of tenure to citizens, and denying it to non-citizens)
- retards or halts the progressive realization of a right, unless it is acting within a limitation permitted by international law (because it lacks resources, or because of unforeseeable and uncontrollable events) (for example, closing all universities during an armed conflict)

A violation occurs either when a state has omitted to act to overcome deprivation or, alternatively, when it has actively impeded, or allowed others to impede, the realization of a right. Violations can be of duties to respect, protect or fulfil rights. Where denial of economic, social and cultural rights is a result of inability (where there are genuine resource constraints, or circumstances beyond the control or outside the knowledge of the state), a state cannot be said to have violated its international obligations. Violations are the result of unwillingness, negligence or discrimination.

Violations of economic, social and cultural rights can therefore occur across the breadth of states' obligations to respect, protect and fulfil human rights. They may include acts of direct obstruction or denial, and failures to act to prevent or redress denial of rights. As is the case for all human rights, many violations involve failures of the state to **desist** from a specific policy, legislative change or practice that is inconsistent with its obligations under international law. Allegations of this sort require proof that the act impedes realization of rights, and that a remedy lies in simply ceasing this course of action. Violations also often involve abuses by other actors, where the state has failed to regulate their conduct and has failed to ensure effective remedies for potential victims.

Allegations of failures to fulfil rights are harder to assess, as fulfilment of economic, social and cultural rights is more dependent on available resources. Nevertheless, three types of violations of the duty to fulfil economic, social and cultural rights can be identified:

- **retrogression**, which includes:
  o developing and implementing new policies that move further from the full realization of rights
  o large-scale disinvestment in social services not justified by a general economic downturn
  o the reallocation of resources away from economic, social and cultural rights to other areas, such as unwarranted or excessive military expenditure

- **discriminatory non-fulfilment**. Non-discrimination is an immediate obligation that cuts across all obligations to respect, protect and fulfil rights. The adoption of laws, policies and practice that are inconsistent with the principle of non-discrimination amounts to a human rights violation.

- the **failure to prioritize minimum core obligations**, particularly for the most vulnerable, when deciding on action to fulfil rights is a human rights violation. In the Democratic Republic of the Congo, South Africa and Swaziland, Amnesty International has concentrated its campaigning on the duty to prioritize health care provision for rape survivors, particularly in the context of the HIV/AIDS pandemic.[106]

Other violations of the duty to fulfil may be more difficult to determine. Whether a state is in violation of its international obligations may involve judgements about resource allocation and policy prioritization. In adjudicating on such matters, courts in some countries have been reticent to intrude on the terrain of the executive or other public policy makers, or to issue rulings implying the redistribution of resources from one sector at the expense of another. However the standard of "reasonableness", developed in the South African courts, is useful in setting a threshold for acceptable state conduct:

> "A Court considering reasonableness will not enquire whether other more desirable or favourable measures could have been adopted, or whether public money could have been better spent. The question would be whether the measures that have been adopted are reasonable. It is necessary to recognise that a wide range of possible measures could be adopted by the State to meet its obligations. Many of these would meet the requirement of reasonableness. Once it is shown that the measures do so, this requirement is met."[107]

In applying this principle, the Constitutional Court of South Africa considered whether the policy or programme was comprehensive, coherent and coordinated; balanced and flexible; allowed for short, medium and long-term needs; was reasonably conceived and implemented; and was transparent.[108]

The Court considered that the obligation to fulfil the right to adequate housing was violated where housing policy did not prioritize the improvement of the housing condition of those living "with no access to land, no roof over their heads, and who were living in intolerable conditions or crisis situations."[109]

States use a variety of arguments to excuse conduct that would generally be considered a human rights violation, often citing insufficient resources or security concerns, the burden of debt repayments or natural disasters. Although states have differing access to resources, international standards on economic, social and cultural rights take this into account: failure to ensure rights that genuinely results from inability cannot be judged a violation.

Thus a temporary closure of a school or hospital following a natural disaster may be understandable where the building must be checked for safety or there are short-term problems in transporting staff to work. However, disaster response must not discriminate against marginalized groups.[110]

Armed conflict is no pretext

Armed conflict or states of emergency often result in widespread violations of economic, social and cultural rights. Health services, housing, food and clean water sources are destroyed or people are prevented from accessing them. Measures to respond to security concerns must be reasonable and proportionate to the threat. In times of armed conflict, they must also respect the distinction between civilians and combatants.

During an armed conflict, or an emergency that "threatens the life of the nation", governments may derogate from (declare that the guarantees are temporarily suspended) some, although not all, human rights obligations.[111] Yet many recent human rights instruments do not contain a derogation clause. In the case of the African Charter, for example, the African Commission on Human and Peoples' Rights has said that "limitations on the rights and freedoms enshrined in the Charter cannot be justified by emergencies or special circumstances."[112]

While the realization of economic, social and cultural rights may be a greater challenge during armed conflict, there is no provision made for derogation from obligations under the International Covenant on Economic, Social and Cultural Rights or other core treaties protecting these rights. As with human rights generally, only reasonable and proportionate limitations on the exercise of economic, social and cultural rights are permitted under international law and in pursuit of a legitimate aim (for example, public health, order and security).

At the very least, states must comply with minimum core obligations, which have been explicitly considered non-derogable.[113]

There are also a series of duties in international humanitarian law – the law of armed conflict – relating to the means and methods of conducting hostilities, and to the duties of an occupying power, which are relevant to economic, social and cultural rights. Examples include:

- the prohibition of starvation as a means of warfare[114]

- the prohibition of means and methods of warfare likely to cause widespread, long-term damage to the environment, thereby jeopardizing the health or survival of the population

A congenitally blind child with her father, Ghifran, Iraq, 2000. Her condition is believed to be connected to the use of depleted uranium munitions by Allied forces in 1991, after the Gulf War. Amnesty International has called for a moratorium on the use of depleted uranium weapons until there are authoritative conclusions on their long-term effects on human health and the environment.

- the prohibition of attack on objects essential to the survival of the civilian population[115]

- the duty to allow the free passage of medical workers and supplies through sieges[116]

- the duty of occupying powers to ensure and maintain medical services, public health and hygiene in territory under occupation[117]

'A part of our lives has gone': destruction of homes and livelihoods in the Israeli-Occupied Territories

"We were stunned. All we had time for was to get the children to safety. By the time we had done that, within a few minutes the bulldozers began destroying the house and there was no time to salvage anything."

Yusuf Muhammad Abu Houli, his wife and their nine children were in their home when it was surrounded by tanks and bulldozers. On 10 October 2000 the Israeli army began to destroy some of their land, and on 26 October demolished the first of the family's houses. On 9 November, a nephew, 'Abd al-Hakim 'Abedrabbo Abu Houli, married with four children, had his house demolished.

"The work of years smashed up just like that. The army came at 11pm with two tanks, one bulldozer and one jeep. They shouted at us to get out immediately or they would tear the house down over our heads. Our house was not the first to be demolished but still, you can't really be prepared for something like that. We had no idea that this was just the beginning, that within a few months we would be left with nothing. It's not just the houses, the furniture, the land, everything. It's a part of our lives which has gone."

Within a year, the extended family had lost a total of nine houses, about 35 hectares of land, a food-processing factory, a plant nursery, a chicken farm, three wells and several water storage pools. In all, 84 relatives were affected and 57 made homeless.

The Israeli army gave no explanation for the destruction of these properties. The family lived near the Israeli settlement of Kfar Darom in the Gaza Strip. In the Gaza Strip alone, some 18,000 Palestinians have been made homeless as the army and security forces have destroyed more than 3,000 homes, vast areas of agricultural land and hundreds of other properties since September 2000.

This massive destruction cannot be justified on the grounds of "absolute military necessity", as the Israeli authorities claim, and is frequently a form of collective punishment in reprisal for attacks by armed groups, in violation of international humanitarian law.[118] The house destructions are carried out without notice, without due process, and without the provision of adequate alternative accommodation. As such, they also amount to forced evictions, which violate a range of human rights, including the right to adequate housing.

Insufficient resources are no excuse

All too frequently, states seek to justify a violation of economic, social and cultural rights on the grounds that they lack financial, technical or human resources.

In considering such claims, it is important to look at whether the state has given sufficient priority to human rights when setting budgets and has genuinely sought international assistance where needed.

Two further basic principles apply. "Even where the available resources are demonstrably inadequate, the obligation remains for a State Party to ensure the widest possible enjoyment of the relevant rights under the prevailing circumstances."[119]

In addition, "even in times of severe resource constraints, whether caused by a process of adjustment, of economic recession, or by other factors, the vulnerable members of society can and indeed must be protected by the adoption of relatively low-cost targeted programmes."[120]

A general lack of resources must also be differentiated from the ability to realize a specific duty. For example, in the course of analysing the adequacy of mental health care in Gambia, the government disclosed that it actually had a sufficient supply of medicines for mental health patients, but that they had not been distributed. Consequently the African Commission on Human and Peoples' Rights could justifiably order that the state provide these medicines to those who had need of them, even though it noted the state's severe resource constraints.[121]

Courts in some jurisdictions have considered whether resources allocation is consistent with constitutional human rights obligations. When the government of South Africa claimed that it lacked resources to provide anti-retroviral drugs to pregnant women, the Constitutional Court did not accept the claim. The Court's position was that the government could not argue that it lacked the resources to provide the drugs without developing a plan to determine the cost of "rolling out" provision across the country as part of a programme for people living with HIV/AIDS, and without assessing the various resources at its disposal.[122]

India: using the courts to defend rights

The right to food has recently been defended in India using public interest litigation. In 2001 several Indian states faced a second or third year of drought but failed to ensure the minimum nutritional requirements of the population despite holding millions of tonnes of food stock. In response to a petition by the People's Union for Civil Liberties and other human rights groups, the Supreme Court first ordered the states to ensure the food needs of "the aged, infirm, disabled, destitute women, destitute men who are in danger of starvation, pregnant and lactating women and destitute children, especially in cases where they or members of their family do not have sufficient funds to provide food for them."[123] States were further directed to reopen food distribution shops and identify those below the poverty line who were in need of food assistance. The court thus required the immediate realization of minimum core obligations of the right to adequate food.[124]

The development of economic, social and cultural rights case law in India is a positive example of creative judicial intervention working from unpromising material. The Indian Constitution makes a distinction between fundamental rights (civil and political rights enforceable in the courts) and directive principles of state policy (to guide governmental decision-making). The Supreme Court, however, has used these principles to broaden the interpretation of fundamental rights. In particular, it has interpreted the right to life to include the right to a livelihood, to adequate nutrition, clothing and reading facilities, and to housing, health and education. Access to the courts for disadvantaged people has been made much easier, through relaxing procedural rules to permit public interest litigation on the basis of informal petitions.

5. Who is responsible?

"In the interest of ensuring that ESC rights are taken more seriously as obligations, international human rights organizations should not be unduly limited in identifying the targets of their naming and the means of their shaming."
Mary Robinson, former UN High Commissioner for Human Rights[125]

Responsibility for denial of economic, social and cultural rights frequently lies not only with governments but also with individuals, groups and enterprises.

Primary accountability in international law rests with the state in whose jurisdiction the violation occurs. However, in situations such as occupation or internal armed conflict, where an occupying state or an armed group exercises effective control over a part of the population, the controlling power should be answerable for human rights abuses within that territory.[126]

During armed conflict, not only states but also other armed groups have responsibilities relating to economic, social and cultural rights under international humanitarian law. For example, Amnesty International issued several open letters to the Communist Party of Nepal (CPN) (Maoist) in 2004. They expressed concern about the impact of abducting schoolchildren for political education on their right to education; and about the potential harm of the Maoists' "blockade" of Kathmandu on access to food and essential medical supplies by the civilian population.[127]

"Stop making profit out of people's lives." Marchers in Durban, South Africa, demand that companies' drugs to treat HIV/AIDS are affordable during the 13th International AIDS Conference, July 2000.

Where an interim UN administration exercises effective or joint control over a territory, it may be responsible for human rights abuses committed in that territory. Amnesty International has called on the UN Interim Mission in Kosovo (UNMIK) and the Kosovo/a authorities to find alternative accommodation for Romani communities living in dangerously polluted settlements.[128]

States are also responsible for abuses by private individuals and other non-state entities, such as transnational corporations, where the state has jurisdiction over such individuals and enterprises, and where it fails to exercise due diligence in regulating their conduct.[129]

The largest 300 firms control about 25 per cent of the world's productive assets.[130] Given this reality, there is an emerging international consensus, supported by Amnesty International, on the need to recognize corporate accountability for human rights abuses. While the primary responsibility lies with states, the Universal Declaration of Human Rights recognizes duties of "every organ of society", including corporations. There are moves to develop international standards that would hold businesses to account for abuses of human rights directly resulting from their operations, and would recognize their duty to prevent such abuses within their sphere of influence.[131]

States that provide international development assistance and cooperation should be held responsible for the human rights impact of their policies outside their borders. Donor states should ensure that their development cooperation policies are consistent with their human rights obligations, not only on paper but also in practice. Those receiving development assistance also have an obligation to ensure that this is used in a way consistent with human rights, including through devoting the maximum available resources towards the full realization of economic, social and cultural rights. Human rights violations resulting from development projects are therefore the responsibility both of donor states – where they were aware or should reasonably have been aware of the implications of the project – and of aid recipient states – where they failed to exercise due diligence to ensure that the intervention was consistent with human rights.

International financial institutions, such as the World Bank, exert enormous influence in defining states' economic and social policies. A particularly controversial aspect of the World Bank's activities is its responsibility and international accountability for the human rights impact of its operations.[132] Officials of the Bank consider that it is not mandated to consider human rights in lending decisions, only economic criteria. Yet, as a specialized agency of the UN, the Bank is composed of states that have responsibilities to respect, protect and fulfil human rights in all activities, including in their actions and decisions taken through the Bank.[133]

Structural Adjustment Programmes, which flourished under the auspices of the World Bank and the International Monetary Fund in the 1980s and early 1990s, united human rights groups and other sectors of civil society in opposition to the reduction of public funding for social services. Under many of the programmes, charges (user fees) were introduced for primary health care and education.[134] The impact on access to primary education, for example, was huge.[135] The capacity of the poor to access these services was significantly reduced, and the World Bank eventually amended its policy. Currently the Bank "does not support user fees for primary education and for basic health services for poor people."[136] To re-introduce free primary education for all, not only those considered poor, will require resources to fill any funding gap. Support from the international donor community would help offset the damage done previously when it encouraged moves away from free provision. International human rights law clearly states that primary education should be free and compulsory.[137]

The most recent attempt to agree a compact for development between international financial institutions and loan recipient states has been the introduction of poverty reduction strategy papers (PRSPs). PRSPs, initiated in 1999 by the World Bank and the International Monetary Fund, are formulated by governments as a condition for debt relief, and are increasingly controversial. As the UN Special Rapporteur on the right to health has noted:

> *"Very few PRSPs built in any health indicators that would monitor the impact on poor people or regions. No PRSPs contained plans to include poor people in a participatory monitoring process. All of these shortcomings would have been, at least, attenuated if the right to health had been taken fully into account during the formulation of the relevant PRSP. It is no surprise that* [a World Health Organization study] *found that no PRSP mentioned health as a human right."*[138]

The potential for PRSPs to mobilize international solidarity through providing a framework for integrating human rights concerns into poverty reduction policies is largely unfulfilled. While some efforts have provided an outline of how this might be achieved, this has yet to be fully implemented in practice.[139]

Participation, monitoring and recording in Ghana

In June 2001 a flood deluged the Nima-Mamobi neighbourhood of Accra, Ghana's capital, with raw sewage. The problem was exacerbated by the failure of local authorities to enforce codes requiring landlords to provide toilets in new homes.

The Legal Resources Centre (LRC), a local human rights body, responded by developing a long-term project to monitor the right to health in the community.[140] They began by surveying 161 households and identified the following priorities:

- affordable health services, particularly the implementation of legal exemptions to user fees
- adequate sanitation services and infrastructure, including toilets, waste-water drainage and rubbish disposal

Addressing the first priority, the LRC adopted a number of strategies. It gathered evidence of violations of the "user fee exemption" law in order to pursue litigation.[141] It worked with health care providers to agree administrative practices to ensure their enforcement of the exemptions, provided community education on the exemptions, and raised its concerns with the government. A memorandum was sent to the World Bank, requesting that it re-evaluate the impact on the right to health in Ghana of its policy on user fees for health care.[142]

On sanitation, the LRC gathered testimonies from members of the community and discussed joint strategies with community leaders, which resulted in the development of a potential litigation strategy. Youth club members and university students started to monitor the maintenance of government-owned toilets, and the frequency of refuse collection and gutter clearance.[143] This evidence was used to support a complaint to the Accra Metropolitan Assembly.

The LRC continues to follow up on each of these strategies, acting as an "anchor non-governmental organization" as part of Accra's inclusion in the UNDP/Peoples' Decade for Human Rights "World Human Rights Cities Project".[144]

Human rights organizations are increasingly adept at highlighting the range of actors who share responsibility for human rights abuses, while keeping the focus of primary responsibility on the state. This case shows how one organization has developed a methodology to document the impact of a particular project of development cooperation and held various actors to account for the denial of the right to health of communities affected by a flood.

As the realization of economic, social and cultural rights requires the acceptance of an integrated human rights approach to health, education and other social services, within states this requires collaboration across government ministries from agriculture to trade. Human rights advocates – who have traditionally targeted the authorities responsible for law enforcement, the penal system, defence and the judiciary on civil and political rights issues – may face new challenges in approaching a broader governmental, as well as non-governmental, audience.

6. All rights for all people

Human rights apply to all people simply because they are human. Yet some people face particular difficulties in realizing their rights because of who they are. Women, for example, not only face direct discrimination in law, but also the impact of long-standing discrimination implicit in dominant social attitudes and "historically unequal power relations between men and women", which have impeded the achievement of gender equality.[145]

People are discriminated against on a wide range of grounds including their gender, race, ethnicity, lack of citizenship, sexuality, health (particularly those living with HIV/AIDS), poverty or disability. Many people face discrimination on several grounds at once, leading to multiple marginalization.

Social movements working for the rights of women, children, indigenous peoples and other groups have highlighted specific ways in which these groups are economically, socially and culturally disempowered and disadvantaged. They have identified measures needed in law and policy to address this. Their efforts are also reflected in the development of international standards specific to these groups. International standards now recognize not only the duty to immediately prohibit discrimination, but also to ensure that it is progressively eliminated. Special measures or "affirmative action" taken to redress conditions (including pervasive discrimination) that prevent or impair the enjoyment of human rights are not prohibited under international law; in fact they are required.[146] Such measures must be reasonable and objective, have a legitimate aim, and cease when the goal is achieved.[147]

Children

> "If children had a voice they would, rightly and repeatedly, criticize adult society for hypocrisy."
>
> Thomas Hammarberg, former Vice Chair, UN Committee on the Rights of the Child[148]

Children's rights have seized the world's imagination in an unprecedented way. The UN Convention on the Rights of the Child has been ratified by more countries, more quickly than any other international treaty. It is now a binding legal standard for the entire world, with the sole exceptions of Somalia and the USA, the only two countries not to have agreed to it. For the first time in international law, the Convention recognized that children are not the property of their parents, or of anyone else.[149] They are fully-fledged human beings with human rights. The Convention includes the key principle that all decisions made on behalf of a child, whether by the state, by a parent or guardian, or by any other person, must be taken in the best interests of the child. It also protects children's right to express opinions and have them taken into account, according to their developing capacities. Other general principles in the Convention include the right to freedom from discrimination and the right to survival and development.

A key theme in the Convention is the protection of children from abuse and exploitation. Such exploitation can take various forms, but is often economically motivated. Economic exploitation is proscribed.[150] One of the main focuses of child rights activists and the UN Committee on the Rights of the Child has been child labour, although the Committee recognizes that "not all areas where an economic element prevails are necessarily exploitative".[151] There are two key ILO standards in this area: Convention 182, which prohibits the most dangerous forms of child labour, and Convention 138 on the minimum age for employment. According to these standards, children may not work in hazardous jobs below 18 years

Regulating the use of child labour: Portugal

An important regional instrument for the protection of economic, social and cultural rights is the European Social Charter. Since 1995, organizations representing victims have had the right to lodge collective complaints outlining alleged violations of Charter rights. An early case, brought by the International Commission of Jurists (ICJ), alleged that Portugal had failed to effectively regulate the working conditions of a large number of children. The ICJ outlined that:

"the granite industry in the north employs young boys who work unprotected from the granite dust while breaking stones. Children are reported to suffer badly from this work, as their lungs are dangerously coated with granite dust and their backs are badly affected."[152]

The European Committee of Social Rights found that this went beyond "light work", that Portugal was insufficiently regulating the practice of employers in using child labour, and was in breach of the Charter[153] and Portuguese law.[154] The decision appears to have led to improvements, including legislative amendments and increasing the number of labour inspectors, and the experience of the ICJ highlights the importance of local partner organizations monitoring follow-up.[155]

of age, and may perform only "light work", which does not interfere with their education, below the age of 15.[156]

Among innovative provisions of the Convention are those that protect the rights of disabled children (Article 23) and extend cultural rights explicitly to indigenous children (Article 30). The Convention also sets out the duty of the state "in case of need to provide material assistance and support programmes [to parents], particularly with regard to nutrition, clothing and housing."[157]

Women

All universal and regional human rights treaties prohibit discrimination on the basis of sex. Yet women continue to face widespread and systematic inequality in the realization of their economic, social and cultural rights. The UN Development Fund for Women has concluded that women's average wages are less than those of men in all countries where data is available.[158]

States that are party to the Convention on the Elimination of All Forms of Discrimination against Women are obliged to "pursue by all appropriate means and without delay a policy of eliminating discrimination against women".[159] This is a significant challenge. Discriminatory practices towards women are often justified by reference to traditional, historical, religious and cultural attitudes. Factors such as the segregated labour market, disparate social roles in terms of family responsibilities and gender-based violence present additional obstacles to equal achievement of economic, social and cultural rights by women. For example, the traditional assignment to women and girls of the role of primary care-giver in the family restricts women's freedom of movement and consequently their access to paid employment and education.[160] When states fail to give adequate priority to primary education for all, it increases the likelihood that families will decide not to send girls to school. The UN Special Rapporteur on the right to education has pointed out that "years of schooling appear wasted when women do not have access to employment and/or are precluded from becoming self-employed, do not have a choice whether to marry and bear children, or their opportunities for political representation are foreclosed."[161]

A range of obstacles inhibits the realization of women's right to health. Among them are: lack of access to health care and health-related information and education, including in relation to family planning; violence, including sexual violence; and harmful traditional practices. Discrimination and unequal relations between men and women underpin these obstacles.

Land is an essential resource in many contexts to achieve the right to an adequate standard of living, yet women are often denied land, inheritance and housing rights. Furthermore, they may not have access to courts in order to enforce their rights, even where these are nominally guaranteed.

"Women's human rights to land and adequate housing are systematically denied – the majority of the well over one billion inadequately housed persons in the world are women. Yet the most blatant gender-specific violation of such rights is the denial of women's rights to own and inherit housing, land and property. Women throughout the world, after the death of a husband or father, are denied these basic rights and deprived of their homes and lands. The effects are devastating: destitution and homelessness, increased vulnerability to HIV/AIDS infection, physical violence, and other grave violations of women's fundamental human rights."

Centre on Housing Rights and Evictions, *Bringing Equality Home*, Geneva, 2004.

Indigenous peoples

There are an estimated 370 million indigenous people across the world, with an extraordinary diversity of cultures and histories. To be identified as "indigenous" implies certain things in common, including:[162]

- Indigenous peoples have a longstanding relationship to the land on which they live that predates colonization or the formation of the contemporary state.
- Indigenous peoples wish to preserve, continue to develop, and pass along to future generations distinct knowledge systems, practices and ways of living intimately linked to this land.
- Except in a few rare cases, the institutions of the countries in which indigenous peoples live are largely shaped and controlled by other ethnic groups that have come into positions of dominance through colonization or the formation of the contemporary state.

Indigenous peoples seek recognition of their rights both as individuals and as nations or peoples on their own terms, in accordance with their traditions.

The centrality of the relation to land of indigenous peoples to the realization of a wide range of rights is increasingly recognized.[163] Traditional ways of living off the land are central to providing food, medicine and housing to indigenous families and communities, and to maintaining the practices that nourish their spiritual and social lives. Indigenous peoples around the world are seeking formal demarcation of their territories: that is, mapping, marking and protecting their boundaries from unwanted intrusions and ecological destruction.

Indigenous peoples' rights are recognized in the national laws and constitutions of some states and in historic and contemporary treaties between indigenous peoples and states. There is also a trend towards their recognition in international law, including existing instruments such as ILO Convention 169 – the Indigenous and Tribal Peoples Convention (1989); references in general human rights instruments; and discussions of a draft UN Declaration on the Rights of Indigenous Peoples.[164] Current concerns of indigenous peoples include ensuring that the right of all peoples to self-determination applies equally to indigenous peoples.[165] Another focus of concern is the right to free, prior, informed consent on decisions affecting the realization of their rights.[166]

Land rights in Brazil and Nicaragua: contrasting outcomes for indigenous people

"In the Guarani and Kaiowá areas, what happens? A lot of malnutrition. We have no land to plant on. Precisely because of this, there is misery and hunger in our land... We Indians have already taken a decision. If an eviction occurs in these areas in conflict, we will commit suicide. We will commit suicide because we don't mean anything to anyone."

Indigenous leader in a public meeting with a special Brazilian senate commission on indigenous affairs, February 2004.[167]

After centuries of violence to drive indigenous peoples in Brazil off their land, they are still being threatened, attacked and killed, and their protection by the state is inconsistent. Successive governments have failed to deliver on international and constitutional obligations to recognize their land rights fully and finally. The current administration has also been slow to follow through on promises to demarcate and ratify territories. This has contributed to attacks on indigenous communities and forced evictions, aggravating already severe economic and social deprivation. Prospectors, ranchers and logging companies seek to exploit the land's natural resources; landowners claim title to it; and the military cite national security interests to reduce and limit the control of border areas by indigenous communities. Such vested interests use substantial economic and political lobbying powers to delay and block the recognition of indigenous peoples' land rights. As a result of state inaction, indigenous peoples are deprived of the essential resource for the realization of their economic, social and cultural rights – their land.[168]

Protection for indigenous land rights was won in 2001 by the Awas Tingni people living on the Atlantic coast of Nicaragua, in the first binding decision by an international human rights tribunal to explicitly recognize the rights of indigenous peoples over communal land. The Awas Tingni appealed in 1995 to the Inter-American Commission on Human Rights to protect rights under threat from logging operations by a foreign company. Although the Nicaraguan Constitution recognizes the rights of indigenous peoples over communally held land, the Awas Tingni lands were untitled. The Inter-American Court of Human Rights in August 2001 found that the government had effectively treated the Awas Tingni land as state property when it granted the logging concession without the consent of the community. It found that Nicaragua had violated the Awas Tingni's rights to judicial proceedings and to property under the American Convention on Human Rights. It ordered the government to refrain from infringing their rights and to ensure the demarcation and titling of all indigenous land.[169]

The inextricable link between culture and other human rights was recognized by the UN Human Rights Committee in a number of decisions concerning the lands and livelihoods of indigenous peoples, including decisions about Lubicon trappers in Canada[170] and Saami reindeer herders in Finland.[171]

Migrants

The ILO estimates that up to 86 million people are economically active outside their country of origin or citizenship.[172] Migrant workers play a vital role in sustaining the economy and enriching the culture in the countries in which they work. Yet people who leave their country for social and economic reasons are often vilified. Many experience discrimination, racism and xenophobia, exploitation and other violations of their human rights, including their economic, social and cultural rights. Many migrants around the world have no status in the country in which they live because they do not have the legal right to enter into or remain in the country. Such people are additionally vulnerable to abuse. Some states are only too willing to turn a blind eye to large numbers of irregular migrant workers working in the informal economy.

Many migrant workers live and work in appalling conditions, without access even to essential services such as health care. The countries of origin of many migrant workers often sign agreements with countries of employment in which their citizens are treated as commodities or mere units of labour. Irregular migrants, who often face expulsion from the state in which they reside, are often unwilling to speak up against abuses of their rights by governments, state agents, or employers, increasing their vulnerability to exploitation.

All migrants, regardless of their status, are entitled to the protection of international human rights law and standards. While the fundamental principle of non-discrimination permits certain distinctions to be made between nationals and non-nationals, these distinctions must serve a legitimate objective and must not be disproportionate. Most importantly, such distinctions must not inhibit the individual, either directly or indirectly, from enjoying his or her human rights. The Committee on the Elimination of Racial Discrimination (which monitors states' compliance with the International Convention on the Elimination of All Forms of Racial Discrimination) recently clarified the scope of the rights of non-citizens. It underlined that the Convention requires, among other things the "Remov[al of] obstacles that prevent the enjoyment of economic, social and cultural rights by non-citizens, notably in the areas of education, housing, employment and health."[173]

The protection of the human rights of migrants is now complemented by the seventh core international human rights treaty, the Migrant Workers Convention.[174] The Convention covers rights and protection for migrant workers at all stages of migration, and applies specific protection to irregular migrants and their families. Amnesty International is campaigning for ratification of the Convention as well as for migrants' rights in specific situations around the world. Amnesty International has for example called on Thailand to respect the rights of migrants from Myanmar, focusing on their rights at work.[175]

Refugees and internally displaced people

There are almost 40 million displaced people in the world: roughly one third of these, 13 million, have left their countries to find protection from conflict or other situations where they would be at risk of serious human rights violations, and are called refugees.[176] Two thirds, around 25 million, are trying to find protection within their country's borders and are known as internally displaced persons.[177] Enjoyment of economic, social and cultural rights is of fundamental importance for refugees and internally displaced people before, during and after their flight.

The denial of economic, social and cultural rights can cause displacement. Massive violations of rights such as the right to food through sieges or discriminatory distribution of food aid can force thousands to leave their homes.[178] Sometimes individuals are specifically targeted: if a state violates the rights of individuals because of who they are (for example, gender, ethnicity) or what they believe in (for example, their religion or political opinions, including opinions on gender roles), this may constitute a ground for recognition as a refugee. The interdependence of rights means that the denial of economic, social and cultural rights is often linked to the denial of civil and political rights.

The current international system for the protection of refugees is based on the 1951 UN Convention relating to the Status of Refugees and its 1967

Children share a school book in a camp for families fleeing the killings in Darfur, western Sudan. Nearly two million people have been displaced by the conflict in Darfur since early 2004, in which thousands of people have been killed by government forces and allied militias. Lack of access to education for their children is a major concern for many displaced people.

Protocol, which aim to ensure that refugees have "the widest possible exercise" of all rights recognized in the Universal Declaration of Human Rights. This requires that states ensure work, housing and education to refugees on their territory on at least as favourable a basis as either nationals or other non-nationals. In countries of asylum, this is now complemented by international law protecting the rights of non-nationals generally.[179]

There are three possible solutions to the plight of refugees: complete local integration in the country of asylum; resettlement in a third country; or voluntary repatriation in safety and dignity to the country of origin. Each requires that refugees are able to enjoy economic, social and cultural rights:

- Refugees who are denied fundamental human rights, including employment and education, in a country of asylum will often need to be resettled to another country where they can realize these rights.

- Denial of economic, social and cultural rights can result in a refugee population failing to integrate for generations.[180] Refugees who are not able to enjoy such fundamental rights as the right to adequate food and clean water, or to work or education, may have no choice but to move onwards of their own accord to another country where they believe they can realize their economic, social and cultural rights.

- Voluntary repatriation will lead to renewed displacement if returnees are not able to rebuild their lives in a sustainable manner, which means they must be able to realize economic, social and cultural rights.[181]

Economic, social and cultural rights are not only important in the long-term perspective. Emergency delivery of food, shelter and health care to displaced populations is an element of states' obligations to realize minimum essential levels of economic, social and cultural rights. According to agreed standards, humanitarian response to emergency situations is premised on the imperative of meeting human needs and restoring human dignity.[182] Often the displaced people themselves will highlight the necessity of realizing economic, social and cultural rights. Many people from Darfur in western Sudan, whom Amnesty International met as refugees in eastern Chad, said that their main concern was that their children should have access to education.[183]

There is no specific international treaty aimed at providing protection for internally displaced people. Many of the main provisions and principles of relevance to their protection and assistance are collected in the UN Guiding Principles on Internal Displacement, a 1998 document that has received widespread endorsement, although it is not legally binding.[184] The Guiding Principles reiterate that the primary responsibility for protection and assistance lies with the state on whose territory the displaced population finds itself. They stipulate the right of all internally displaced people to an adequate standard of living, and to certain minimum economic, social and cultural rights "regardless of the circumstances, and without discrimination". They also contain standards on the necessity of access to displaced populations for humanitarian organizations to deliver assistance, and the obligations of humanitarian organizations to respect the human rights of the internally displaced people.

7. Defending economic, social and cultural rights

Human rights are recognized as a result of popular struggles. It is people, not politicians, who claim rights, and it is their efforts that lead to official recognition. All significant advances in the protection of human rights have developed from social struggles, including those of organized labour, anti-colonialists, the women's movement and indigenous peoples.

Campaigning against abuses of economic, social and cultural rights is not new. Local, national and regional human rights organizations have been defending these rights for decades. International organizations working on these rights emerged from the 1980s onwards, including the international Food First Information and Action Network (FIAN) in 1986, the Center on Economic and Social Rights in 1993, the Centre on Housing Rights and Evictions (COHRE) in 1994, and many others. There is now a broad international network of economic, social and cultural rights NGOs (ESCR-NET). Yet scepticism on the nature of these rights persists, particularly on how to campaign against their violation. Some people within the international human rights movement question to what extent international human rights organizations should work on these issues.[185]

Students and civil society activists join a protest by members of AI Nepal in Kathmandu on behalf of the victims of the Bhopal chemical disaster in India, 16 May 2005. Amnesty International called on Dow Chemical Company to clean up the site more than 20 years after a toxic gas leak killed over 20,000 people.

Key challenges for those campaigning to advance economic, social and cultural rights include identifying violations, victims, violators and remedies on which to focus campaigning. How best can human rights activists transform calls for policy reforms into concrete actions that highlight the need for change to improve the lives of individuals, groups and communities?

Working effectively to promote greater respect for economic, social and cultural rights will often mean confronting structural failings and underlying factors that allow individual abuses to continue. This is true for all human rights campaigning. Such changes may be as relatively straightforward as legislative amendments. They can also be as challenging as seeking to alter entrenched patterns of abuse, where methods include human rights training programmes for the police, prosecutors and judges, or for health professionals, food distributors, educators and policy makers.

One way of opposing violations of economic, social and cultural rights is to expose the impact of policies, projects and action that deprive individuals and groups of the ability to realize their rights.

Working for change through individual cases

For over 40 years, Amnesty International has mobilized millions of people all over the world to oppose human rights abuses. Largely, this has been through telling the stories of real women, men and children, and giving a human face to statistics of atrocities and neglect. The accounts of individuals who have suffered violations of their economic, social and cultural rights can be told equally effectively to highlight the impact of government action or inaction. While demanding remedies for a particular individual or group at risk, broader systemic factors can also be challenged.

Urgent appeals for individuals and a community at risk in Mexico

When Margarito de la Cruz Ortiz, Paulino Díaz and other members of the community of San Rafael in Mexico were under threat, members of Amnesty International's Urgent Action network sprang into action.[186] The isolated village had been badly damaged in a landslide in 2003. Many families were left homeless or sleeping in temporary shelters. Others were said to be living in houses at serious risk of collapse. When community leaders complained to human rights groups of official failures to rehouse them, soldiers and police officers visited the village, apparently in an attempt to intimidate the community. Local people reported their predicament to the UN Special Rapporteur on the right to adequate housing and appealed to the Inter-American Commission on Human Rights for interim measures to prevent irreparable harm. Amnesty International members called for an investigation into the role of the military and police, and for the authorities to address the community's complaints of unsafe and inadequate housing.

In early 2005 the community was rehoused and provided with access to clean drinking water, sanitation and shelter. In April 2005, Amnesty International representatives were invited to the inauguration of the community's new settlement, and the community decided to name streets in their new village after each of the organizations which had helped them in their campaign.

Taking on the drug companies and the government in South Africa

The Southern African region has been one of the worst affected by the HIV/AIDS pandemic. In South Africa, an estimated 5 million people – some 10 per cent of the population – are now HIV positive, with 600 people thought to die of AIDS-related illnesses every day.

The Treatment Action Campaign (TAC) was launched in 1998 to campaign for greater access to HIV treatment, by raising public awareness and understanding about issues surrounding the availability, affordability and use of HIV treatments.[187] To achieve its goals, TAC:

- formed professional alliances with activist economists, doctors and lawyers to research and present its case to drug companies, to the government, and ultimately in court
- undertook a five-year public education programme on treatment literacy to compensate for poorly trained health professionals and under-resourced facilities
- formed alliances with labour and religious sectors in launching its campaign, in the face of strong ideological disagreements

In 1998, a group of pharmaceutical companies took the government of South Africa to court to oppose draft legislation that would have allowed compulsory licensing and parallel import of anti-retroviral drugs, greatly reducing the cost of the drugs and allowing more people access to treatment. TAC and a global alliance of civil society organizations "named and shamed" the drug companies involved in the litigation, and campaigned in the companies' home countries, notably Switzerland and the USA. Faced with a growing international backlash, and the possibility of an unfavourable precedent in the South African Constitutional Court, the pharmaceutical companies eventually withdrew their claim in 2001.

TAC then found that this victory alone was insufficient. The government appeared reluctant to extend even its mother to child transmission prevention (MTCTP) scheme beyond 18 pilot sites. It cited cost, safety fears over the drugs, a need for counselling during the treatment course as well as infrastructure failures in the health service as reasons for stalling on the "rollout" of the provision of anti-retroviral drugs. TAC took the case to court. In December 2001 the Pretoria High Court accepted TAC's arguments and ordered the government to develop a plan of how it would extend the MTCTP scheme by March 2002.

The court determined that government policy prohibiting the use of one drug, nevirapine, outside the pilot sites was an unreasonable limitation on the duty to progressively realize the right to health. The court concluded that the government was under a duty to develop a plan to roll out MTCTP across the country, and then to address how to mobilize resources.[188]

As the government delayed on implementing this decision, TAC organized a series of protests, marches, complaints to the South African Human Rights Commission, letter-writing, and finally a campaign of civil disobedience called

"Dying for Treatment". By mid-2003, there appeared to be significant progress towards rolling out anti-retroviral drug treatment. Following tests for safety of key drugs, in August the government finally signed an agreement with the Global Fund to Fight AIDS, Tuberculosis and Malaria which provided US$41 million for the HIV treatment plan. The following day the government instructed the health department to develop a detailed operational plan for the anti-retroviral drug rollout.

The manufacturers of more than half the world's anti-HIV drugs (GlaxoSmithKline and Boehringer Ingelheim) receive compensation from the government of South Africa in return for permitting the production of generic versions of the drugs in South Africa. This was agreed after TAC filed a complaint with South Africa's Competition Commission. Had the complaint been considered by the competition tribunal, the companies would have been required to indicate the true cost of research and development of the drugs. TAC continues to monitor government progress in rolling out provision of anti-retroviral drugs.[189]

Documenting abuses

While developing indicators of progress or decline in the realization of economic, social and cultural rights is an enduring challenge to the human rights community, research into violations of these rights is in many cases similar to research into violations of civil and political rights.

Campaigning strategies can be based on documenting abuses of governments' duties to respect or protect rights – such as forced eviction, poisoning water supplies, and crop destruction. They can also be built on identifying the people affected and the remedies required, such as halting the abuse and providing adequate reparation, and on identifying the range of actors responsible, such as a polluting business and the state that fails to regulate the activities of its businesses, at home and abroad. Campaigning tactics such as letter-writing and publicity can have success in such cases.

Skills in documenting economic, social and cultural rights are developing. They are increasingly shared internationally, through international workshops and networks, in manuals by NGOs for NGOs,[190] and through skills sharing on techniques ranging from budgetary analysis to the use of the constitution to effect change. Links between organizations working for economic, social and cultural rights around the world have never been stronger. One of the strengths of joining national campaigns with international solidarity is the ability to highlight the international dimensions of states' obligations towards economic, social and cultural rights, and how actions abroad, whether by the state, its representatives (including multilateral development banks) or its businesses, impact on the realization of human rights.

The indivisibility of all human rights often emerges when human rights organizations document patterns of human rights violations. The imprisonment of people campaigning for recognition of their land rights; the use of disproportionate force in response to protests over the impact of water privatization; the lack of judicial independence in eviction cases – all demand a holistic human rights response.

Public hearings in India and Thailand

Human rights standards guarantee the right to seek, receive and impart information.[191] While this has long been used by journalists, more recently social movements have used this right to seek information on budgetary allocations in order to hold local officials accountable.

In Thailand, the Assembly of the Poor brings together development professionals, government representatives, human rights organizations and community representatives to discuss the impact of development interventions. The Assembly reportedly led to some projects being cancelled, facilitated the participation of communities in drafting relevant legislation to protect their rights, and obtained compensation for those already affected.[192]

In India, the Mazdoor Kisan Shakti Sangathan (Union for Empowerment of Peasants and Labourers, MKSS), a grassroots organization in the state of Rajasthan, organizes Jan Sunwais (People's Hearings), where official documents about development projects are read aloud to villagers. Villagers then point out inaccuracies, such as the inclusion of dead people, records of allegedly completed projects that in fact never began, and inflated claims of food distribution.

Officials and contractors are invited to the hearings, where they answer questions and give their account. Although there has seldom been criminal action taken against corrupt officials, in some cases they have returned money after being exposed.[193] As two founders of MKSS state, "The right to information has...taken away the protection provided by secrecy to carry out...misdeeds in the name of development."[194]

The work of MKSS and similar organizations in India was boosted by the Supreme Court, which held that "people at large have a right to know in order to take part in participatory development in the industrial life and democracy."[195]

A National Campaign for the People's Right to Information in 1997 eventually contributed to the passing of legislation that secured the right to information in Rajasthan and several other Indian states, and discussion of a guaranteed right to information at the national level.[196]

Working in partnership

"By working in collaboration or partnership with local civil society organizations, international human rights organizations can strengthen the hand of these organizations and also obtain... legitimacy of voice"

Mary Robinson, former UN High Commissioner for Human Rights[197]

International human rights organizations new to working on economic, social and cultural rights have much to learn from those local, national, regional and international human rights and other civil society organizations with greater experience of documenting and campaigning on these issues.

Many community based organizations, indigenous peoples, development organizations and other civil society representatives have long campaigned for social justice concerns which can be defined as human rights issues. The human rights movement and other movements for social justice have much to learn from one another, and regional and international Social Forums may continue to offer a key opportunity for sharing experience and perspectives.

Groups promoting economic, social and cultural rights have used a range of approaches and initiatives and have joined in broad partnerships to advance their goals. They have worked with legislators and lawyers to draft legislation, have initiated court cases on behalf of individuals or groups, and have increased media and public interest in significant cases. They have trained law enforcement officers, judges and others on economic, social and cultural rights. Others have held public hearings and used the right to information to challenge the corrupt diversion of resources that should have been used to realize economic, social and cultural rights. Other techniques include demanding recognition of economic, social and cultural rights in legislation and especially the constitution, long-term grassroots monitoring and budgetary analysis.

Lobbying for constitutional guarantees

"A Constitution containing only civil and political rights projects an image of truncated humanity. Symbolically, but still brutally, it excludes those segments of society for whom autonomy means little without the necessities of life."[198]

Lobbying for amendments to legislation and constitutions so that they reflect all human rights obligations of the state is a growing area of human rights advocacy. Some economic, social and cultural rights (such as the right to education) are included in a large number of constitutions.[199] Others (such as the right to water) have only recently begun to be systematically included in constitutions in response to campaigning and outrage at their violation.[200] Inclusion of economic, social and cultural rights in the constitution does not guarantee their respect, but it represents an important commitment to the indivisibility of human rights and facilitates the enforcement of these rights by affected people.

A number of constitutions safeguard minimum resource allocation for the realization of economic, social and cultural rights. The constitutions of Brazil, Costa Rica and the Philippines, for example, have been used to challenge budgetary allocations for education, in the courts through public interest litigation and on the streets through direct action to demand compliance with constitutional obligations.

Examining budgets

"Budget analysis can often pinpoint inadequacies in expenditures, misdirection of funds or a 'misfit' of expenditures relative to the government's stated human rights commitments – particularly with regard to its 'positive' obligations (obligations to take action) rather than its 'negative' obligations (obligations to desist from doing something)."[201]

Budgetary analysis is fast emerging as a key technique in pressing governments to meet their human rights obligations. Particularly for economic, social and cultural rights, this method allows human rights activists to quantify the steps the government is taking to fulfil its obligations. As a parallel process to documenting violation and abuse, it can be a significant tool in monitoring and encouraging the progressive realization of rights.[202]

Time for action

There can no longer be any excuses for failing to take action. Violations of people's economic, social and cultural rights can no longer be ignored. Hunger, homelessness and preventable disease can no longer be treated as

An activists' task list

Human rights advocates, gathered together in the mid-1990s, identified the following tasks as key to documenting and campaigning for economic, social and cultural rights:[203]

- identifying the rights issues of immediate concern to the country or community
- monitoring the state's development of the conditions necessary to ensure economic, social and cultural rights and, in particular, its implementation of related policies, plans and legislation
- monitoring, documenting and reporting on the government's actions in complying with, or violating, its obligations
- observing the government's compliance with recommendations made by international human rights bodies. This would include first-hand collection of facts and evidence from various sources
- ascertaining the availability of legal remedies, and determining their enforceability under national laws. This would involve researching the relevant laws and analysing court decisions related to economic, social and cultural rights claims
- responding to individual or community complaints of violations
- educating the population on their economic, social and cultural rights, and
- mobilizing and collaborating with communities and other organizations in advocacy[204]

though they were intractable social problems or solely the product of natural disasters – they are a human rights scandal.

Deprivation of rights cannot be blamed on lack of resources alone – invariably they result also from lack of political will and from discrimination. In the wealthiest countries, marginalized groups suffer poverty and injustice. In the poorest, the international community has allowed millions of people to suffer the utmost deprivation.

In many countries, governments hide behind the excuse of lack of resources to fail their people, to deny them the means to realize their rights, and to allow companies and others to act without restriction, even where this means endangering the lives and health of the people.

In response, human rights defenders have documented violations and abuses, and launched imaginative campaigns to change policies and practice. They have sought to improve the lives of all and to defend their right to live with dignity. Economic, social and cultural rights are not just aspirations. They are not goals that can be deferred to the future. They are based in international law and enforced by international and national tribunals in an increasing body of case law. They demand immediate respect.

Governments must refrain from undermining people's efforts to realize their rights. They must stop discriminating against marginalized groups and must actively include the excluded. They must regulate corporations and other non-state actors to ensure that they respect human rights. These obligations do not cease at their borders. They extend to their actions abroad, whether alone or through international financial institutions.

This primer shows what can be achieved by determined campaigning. It makes the case that economic, social and cultural rights are an integral part of the human rights agenda. Promoting and defending economic, social and cultural rights should be an urgent priority, not just for individual governments, but for the international community and the human rights movement and civil society as a whole.

Endnotes

1 Annan, K., *In Larger Freedom: towards development, security and human rights for all*, UN Doc. A/59/2005, 2005.

2 Food and Agriculture Organization, *The State of Food Insecurity in the World 2003*.

3 World Health Organization, *WHO and the Millennium Development Goals*, Fact sheet No. 290, May 2005, www.who.int/mediacentre/factsheets/fs290/en/index.html

4 Education for All Global Monitoring Report, 2005, *The Quality Imperative*, UNESCO, www.efareport.unesco.org

5 Amnesty International, *Zimbabwe: Power and hunger – Violations of the right to food* (AI Index: AFR 46/026/2004).

6 Tomaševski, K., "Unasked questions about economic, social and cultural rights from the experience of the Special Rapporteur on the right to education (1998-2004)", Human Rights Quarterly 27 (2005) 713.

7 The Human Rights Committee recognized this aspect of the right to life in General Comment 6, *The right to life*, para 5.

8 *Villagrán Morales and others (street children case)*, decision of 19 November 1999, Series C, Inter-American Court of Human Rights, Opinion of Judges Cançado Trinidade and Abreu-Burelli.

9 Amnesty International, *Israel and the Occupied Territories: Surviving under siege – the impact of movement restrictions on the right to work* (AI Index: MDE 15/001/2003); *The issue of settlements must be addressed according to international law* (AI Index: MDE 15/085/2003); *The place of the fence/wall in international law* (AI Index: MDE 15/016/2004); and *Conflict, occupation and patriarchy – women carry the burden* (AI Index: MDE 15/016/2005).

10 Amnesty International, *Israel and the Occupied Territories: Conflict, occupation and patriarchy – women carry the burden* (AI Index: MDE 15/016/2005).

11 International Human Rights Internship Program and Asian Forum for Human Rights and Development, 2000, p. 13.

12 Vienna Declaration and Programme of Action, UN Doc. A/CONF.157/23, 12 July 1993.

13 Preamble to the Constitution of the International Labour Organization, 1919, http://www.ilo.org/public/english/about/iloconst.htm#pre

14 The Universal Declaration of Human Rights (UDHR) was inspired by President F.D. Roosevelt's "four freedoms" speech to the US Congress on 6 January 1941; Eleanor Roosevelt and French diplomat René Cassin took lead roles in its drafting.

15 Preamble of the UDHR.

16 International Covenant on Economic, Social and Cultural Rights (ICESCR), http://www.unhchr.ch/html/menu3/b/a_cescr.htm

17 Office of the UN High Commissioner for Human Rights (OHCHR), www.ohchr.org. 154 states have ratified the International Covenant on Civil and Political Rights (ICCPR).

18 General Comments are authoritative, although not legally binding, interpretations of obligations under the treaty on the basis of the Committee's understanding of state practice, and can be found at http://www.un.org/search/ohchr_e.htm

19 Drèze, J. and Sen, A., *Hunger and Public Action*, Clarendon Press, Oxford, 1989.

20 African Commission on Human and Peoples' Rights, *Social and Economic Rights Action Center and Center for Economic and Social Rights v Nigeria*, Communication No. 155/96, October 2001.

21 *Guerra and Others v Italy*, European Court of Human Rights, 116/1996/735/932.

22 Additional Protocol to the American Convention on Human Rights (San Salvador Protocol), 1989, which entered into force in 1999; Revised European Social Charter, 1996.

23 Open-ended working group of the Commission on Human Rights to consider options regarding the elaboration of an Optional Protocol to the International Covenant on Economic, Social and Cultural Rights, http://www.ohchr.org/english/issues/escr/group.htm

24 Comments submitted by the USA, report of the Open-ended Working Group on the right to development, UN Doc. E/CN.4/2001/26, cited in Tomaševski, K., "Unasked questions about economic, social and cultural rights from the experience of the Special Rapporteur on the right to education (1998-2004)", Human Rights Quarterly 27 (2005) 713.

25 The CEJIL website is at: www.cejil.org

26 UNDP, *Human Development Report*, 2000, p. 73. See also, "UN Common Understanding of a Human Rights-based Approach to Development Cooperation" cited in UNDP, *Human Rights in the UNDP*, Practice Note, April 2005, p. 16.

27 Alston, P., "A Human Rights Perspective on the Millennium Development Goals." Paper prepared as a contribution to the work of the UN Millennium Project Task Force on Poverty and Economic Development, 2004.

28 See World Bank and IMF Development Committee, *Global Monitoring Report 2004: Policies and Actions for Achieving the MDGs and Related Outcomes*, Washington, DC, 2004.

29 See, for example, the Global Call to Action against Poverty, at www.whiteband.org; Amnesty International, *Guatemala: the Impact of the Free Trade Agreement on human rights should be assessed by Congress* (AI Index: AMR 34/010/2005) and *Memorandum to the Government of Guatemala* (AI Index: AMR 34/014/2005).

30 *Airey v Ireland*, (6289/73) [1979] European Convention for the Protection of Human Rights and Fundamental Freedoms (ECHR) 3, decision of 9 October 1979, para 26.

31 The Committee on the Rights of the Child has indicated that respect for the right to education requires "recognition of the need for a balanced approach to education and one which succeeds in reconciling diverse values through dialogue and respect for difference." General Comment 1, *The aims of education*, UN Doc. CRC/GC/2001/1, para 4.

32 See also Article 17 of the Protocol to the African Charter on Human and Peoples' Rights on the Rights of Women in Africa, on women's "right to a positive cultural context", including their participation in the formulation of cultural policies.

33 See, for example, Communication No. 167/1984, *Lubicon Lake Band v Canada*, UN Doc. Supp. No. 40 (A/45/40) at 1; and Amnesty International, *Canada: "Time is wasting" – Respect for the land rights of the Lubicon Cree long overdue* (AI Index: AMR 20/001/2003).

34 Arab Charter on Human Rights, Article 9(4).

35 Article 24(3), Convention on the Rights of the Child (CRC); Article 21, African Charter on the Rights and Welfare of the Child.

36 World Food Programme, *Tackling Hunger in a World Full of Food*, 1998, section 1.4, at www.wfp.org

37 The right to adequate food: Article 11, ICESCR; Article 24(2)(c), CRC; Article 12, San Salvador Protocol, among others.

38 Committee on Economic, Social and Cultural Rights, General Comment 12, *The right to adequate food*, UN Doc. E/C.12/1999/5, para 6.

39 Committee on Economic, Social and Cultural Rights, General Comment 12, *The right to adequate food*, UN Doc. E/C.12/1999/5, para 36.

40 Amnesty International, *Starved of rights: Human rights and the food crisis in the Democratic People's Republic of Korea (North Korea)* (AI Index: ASA 24/003/2004).

41 Committee on Economic, Social and Cultural Rights, General Comment 12, *The right to adequate food*, UN Doc. E/C.12/1999/5, para 8.

42 African Commission on Human and Peoples' Rights, *Social and Economic Rights Action Center and Center for Economic and Social Rights v Nigeria*, Communication No. 155/96, October 2001.

43 Communication No. 763/1997, *Ms Yekaterina Pavlovna Lantsova v The Russian Federation*, UN Doc. CCPR/C/74/D/763/1997. The ICCPR regulates conditions of all people deprived of their liberty: in prisons, hospitals – particularly psychiatric hospitals, detention camps, correctional institutions or elsewhere (UN Human Rights Committee, General Comment 21 on Article 10, para. 2).

44 Article 12.2, Convention on the Elimination of All Forms of Discrimination against Women (CEDAW); Article 14.2 (b), Protocol to the African Charter on Human and Peoples' Rights on the Rights of Women in Africa.

45 The right to adequate housing: Article 11, ICESCR; 14(2), CEDAW; 16(1) and 27(3), CRC; 5(e)(iii), International Convention on the Elimination of All Forms of Racial Discrimination (ICERD); 17(1), ICCPR; 8(1), ECHR; 8, 11, 23, American Declaration on the Rights and Duties of Man, among others. The scope of the right to adequate housing has been clarified in Committee on Economic, Social and Cultural Rights, General Comment 4, *The right to adequate housing*, UN Doc. E/1992/23, and reports of the UN Special Rapporteur on the right to adequate housing as a component of the right to a decent standard of living.

46 Centre on Housing Rights and Evictions (COHRE), www.cohre.org

47 UN Commission on Human Rights, Resolution 1993/77, March 1993.

48 UN Committee on Economic, Social and Cultural Rights, General Comment 7, *The right to adequate housing*, 20 May 1997, Article 11(1) on forced evictions.

49 The right to education: Articles 13-14, ICESCR; 28-29, CRC; 10, CEDAW; 13, San Salvador Protocol; Protocol 1, ECHR; 11, African Charter on the Rights and Welfare of the Child, among others. The scope of the right to education has been clarified in Committee on Economic, Social and Cultural Rights, General Comment 13, *The right to education*, UN Doc. E/C.12/1999/10, and reports of the UN Special Rapporteur on the right to education.

50 For more information, see the Right to Education Project, www.right-to-education.org

51 Save the Children, *Denied a Future – the right to education of Roma/Gypsy and Traveller Children in Europe*, London, 2001.

52 Concluding observations: Croatia, UN Doc. CRC/C/15/Add.243, 3 November 2004, at www.unhchr.ch. See also Amnesty International, *Briefing to the UN Committee on the Rights of the Child*, 37th session, September 2004 (AI Index: EUR 64/003/2004).

53 The right to health: Article 12, ICESCR; 5 (e) (iv), ICERD; 11.1 (f), CEDAW; 24, CRC; 11, Revised European Social Charter; 16, African Charter on Human and Peoples' Rights; 14, African Charter on the Rights and Welfare of the Child; 10, San Salvador Protocol, among others.

54 Committee on Economic, Social and Cultural Rights, General Comment 14, *The right to health*, UN Doc. E/C.12/2000/4, para 11. The scope of the right to health has also been clarified in the work of the UN Special Rapporteur on the right of everyone to the enjoyment of the highest attainable standard of physical and mental health (Special Rapporteur on the right to health).

55 Committee on Economic, Social and Cultural Rights, General Comment 14, *The right to health*, UN Doc. E/C.12/2000/4.

56 Adapted from Committee on Economic, Social and Cultural Rights, General Comment 14, *The right to health*, UN Doc. E/C.12/2000/4, para 12.

57 Chapman, A., "Violations of the Right to Health", in Netherlands Institute of Human Rights, SIM Special No. 20, 1998.

58 Report of the Special Rapporteur on the right to health, UN Doc. E/CN.4/2005/51.

59 World Health Organization, *World Health Report 2001*, p. 3.

60 Amnesty International, *Guatemala: the Impact of the Free Trade Agreement on human rights should be assessed by Congress* (AI Index: AMR 34/010/2005) and *Memorandum to the Government of Guatemala* (AI Index: AMR 34/014/2005).

61 Amnesty International, *India: Clouds of Injustice: Bhopal disaster 20 years on*, (AI Index: ASA 20/015/2004).

62 Howard, G. and Bartram, J., *Domestic Water Quantity, Service Level and Health*, World Health Organization, 2003, p. 1.

63 World Health Organization/OHCHR, *The right to water*, 2003, p. 6, http://www.who.int/water_sanitation_health/rtwrev.pdf

64 The right to water: Article 11, ICESCR; 24(2), CRC; 14(2), CEDAW; 14(2), African Charter on the Rights and Welfare of the Child, among others. The right to water was recognized as an element of the right to a decent standard of living by the Committee on Economic, Social and Cultural Rights in General Comment 15, *The right to water*, UN Doc. E/C.12/2002/11.

65 Committee on Economic, Social and Cultural Rights, General Comment 15, *The right to water*, UN Doc. E/C.12/2002/11, para 16.

66 The right to work and rights at work: Articles 6-8, ICESCR; 11, CEDAW; 5(e)(i), ICERD; 6-7, San Salvador Protocol; 15, 29(6), African Charter on Human and Peoples' Rights; 1-4 and 8, European Social Charter, among others.

67 Amnesty International, *Myanmar: The Rohingya Minority – Fundamental Rights Denied* (AI Index: ASA 16/005/2004).

68 A General Comment outlining the scope of the right to work is currently under discussion by the Committee on Economic, Social and Cultural Rights.

69 Prohibited in ILO Convention 29 (Article 2(1)). There are several narrow exceptions to this general rule. See also ILO Convention 105.

70 For example, Weigel, George, "Mrs. Roosevelt's confusions revisited", American Purpose, Issue 1, vol.9, 1995.

71 Tomaševski, K., *Preliminary report of the Special Rapporteur on the right to education*, UN Doc. E/CN.4/1999/49, para 41.

72 This typology has now been recognized by treaty monitoring bodies as well as regional human rights enforcement bodies. See General Comments of the Committee on Economic, Social and Cultural Rights and, for example, Inter-American Court of Human Rights, *Case Velázquez Rodríguez*, Judgment of 29 July 1988, Series C, No. 4, and *Social and Economic Rights Action Center and Center for Economic and Social Rights v Nigeria*, African Commission on Human and Peoples' Rights, Communication No. 155/96, October 2001.

73 UN Charter Articles 55 and 56 provide that all members pledge themselves to promote universal respect for, and observance of, human rights and fundamental freedoms for all without distinction.

74 The duty to protect applies to all human rights: Human Rights Committee, General Comment 31 on Article 2, *The Nature of the General Legal Obligation Imposed on States Parties to the Covenant*, UN Doc. HRI/GEN/1/Rev.6, para 8.

75 Cámara Nacional en lo Contencioso-Administrativo Federal, IV, *Viceconte, Mariela C. v El Ministerio de Salud y Acción Social*, 2/6/1998, see http://www.cohre.org/library/Litigating%20ESCR%20Report.pdf

76 ICESCR, Article 2(1).

77 Committee on Economic, Social and Cultural Rights, General Comment 3, *The nature of states parties' obligations*, UN Doc. E/1991/23.

78 Committee on Economic, Social and Cultural Rights, General Comment 3, *The nature of states parties' obligations*, UN Doc. E/1991/23, para 4.

79 Committee on Economic, Social and Cultural Rights, General Comment 3, *The nature of states parties' obligations*, UN Doc. E/1991/23.

80 Committee on Economic, Social and Cultural Rights, General Comment 3, *The nature of states parties' obligations*, UN Doc. E/1991/23.

81 African Commission on Human and Peoples' Rights, *Free Legal Assistance Group, Lawyers Committee for Human Rights, Union Interafricaine des Droits de l'Homme, Les Témoins de Jehovah v Zaire*, Communication Nos. 25/89, 47/90, 56/91 and 100/93 (joined), *Ninth Annual Activity Report of the African Commission on Human and Peoples' Rights 1995/96, Assembly of Heads of State and Government, 32nd Ordinary Session*, 7-10 July, Yaoundé, Cameroon.

82 Committee on Economic, Social and Cultural Rights, General Comment 3, *The nature of states parties' obligations*, UN Doc. E/1991/23 (the examples given are indicative, not exhaustive).

83 Marta Santos Pais (former Chair of the UN Committee on the Rights of the Child and Director of the UNICEF Innocenti Research Centre), *A Human Rights Conceptual Framework for UNICEF*, UNICEF Innocenti Essays No. 9, 1999, p. 8.

84 Committee on Economic, Social and Cultural Rights, General Comment 3, *The nature of states parties' obligations*, UN Doc. E/1991/23, para 12.

85 Annan, K., *We the Peoples: The Role of the United Nations in the 21st Century*, United Nations, 2000.

86 See Coomans, Fons, "Some remarks on the extraterritorial application of the ICESCR" in Coomans and Kamminga (eds.), *Extraterritorial application of human rights treaties*, Intersentia, 2004; Sepúlveda, Magdalena, *The Nature of the Obligations under the ICESCR*, Intersentia, 2003, pp. 370-377; Skogly, Sigrun, and Gibney, Mark, "Transnational Human Rights Obligations", Human Rights Quarterly 24.3 (2002), 781-798; International Council on Human Rights Policy, *Duties Sans Frontières: human rights and global social justice*, 2003.

87 UN Charter Articles 55 and 56.

88 According to its mandate, the Inspection Panel can only take into consideration the Bank's own policies, although it has sometimes also taken relevant human rights principles into account.

89 World Bank, Inspection Panel Report and Recommendation on Request for Investigation, Nigeria: Lagos Drainage and Sanitation Project, http://wbln0018.worldbank.org/IPN/ipnweb.nsf/(attachmentweb)/Lagos_Sanitation_Report/$FILE/Lagos_Sanitation_Report.pdf

90 SERAC, *Expendable People: an Exploratory Report on Planned Forced Evictions in Lagos*, Lagos, 1998, http://www.seracnig.org

91 Frontline Defenders, *ESC Rights: a valid history, a vibrant future*, http://www.frontlinedefenders.org/

92 SERAC, Press Release, 23 October 2003, Lagos, www.seracnig.org

93 Article 2(1), ICESCR, and Article 4, CRC.

94 Recognized explicitly in ICESCR, Article 11.1, in respect of the right to adequate food.

95 For example, in respect of the right to adequate food, "[a] state claiming that it is unable to carry out its obligations for reasons beyond its control therefore has the burden of proving that this is the case and that it has unsuccessfully sought to obtain international support to ensure the availability and accessibility of the necessary food." Committee on Economic, Social and Cultural Rights, General Comment 12, para 17.

96 Committee on Economic, Social and Cultural Rights, General Comment 3, *The nature of states parties' obligations*, UN Doc. E/1991/23, para 14.

97 *Learning Together: The challenge of applying a human rights approach to education – Lessons and suggestions from Zambia*, Norwegian Agency for Development Co-operation (NORAD), 2002.

98 Concluding observations on Ireland (UN Doc. E/C.12/1/Add.77), UK (E/C.12/1/Add.79), France (E/C.12/1/Add.72), Sweden (E/C.12/1/Add.70), Japan (E/C.12/1/Add.67), Germany (E/C.12/1/Add.68) and Finland (E/C.12/1/Add.52); see generally Künnemann, Rolf, "Extraterritorial application of the ICESCR" in Coomans and Kamminga (eds.), *Extraterritorial application of human rights treaties*, Intersentia, 2004.

99 UN Millennium Declaration, adopted by General Assembly Resolution 55/2, 8 September 2000; the Millennium Development Goals, UNDP website, http://www.undp.org/mdg/abcs.html

100 Maastricht Guidelines on Violations of Economic, Social and Cultural Rights, UN Doc. E/C.12/2000/13, para 11.

101 Submission of the Committee on Economic, Social and Cultural Rights to the World Conference on Human Rights, 1993, UN Doc. E/1993/22, Annex III, para 7.

102 See the HURIST (Human Rights Strengthening) Programme, a joint programme of UNDP and OHCHR, at www.ohchr.org

103 Developed in Chapman, Audrey R., "A 'violations approach' for monitoring the ICESCR", Human Rights Quarterly 18 (1996) 23-66.

104 Adapted from The Limburg Principles on the Implementation of the International Covenant on Economic, Social and Cultural Rights (Limburg Principles), UN Doc. E/CN.4/1987/17 (and in E/C.12/2000/13), para 72.

105 The exercise of the rights in the ICESCR may be subject "only to such limitations as are determined by law only in so far as this may be compatible with the nature of these rights and solely for the purpose of promoting the general welfare in a democratic society", Article 4, ICESCR. This article "was primarily intended to be protective of the rights of individuals rather than permissive of the imposition of limitations by the State", Limburg Principles, UN Doc. E/CN.4/1987/17 (and in E/C.12/2000/13), para 46.

106 Amnesty International, *Democratic Republic of Congo, Mass Rape: time for remedies* (AI Index: AFR 62/018/2004); *Amnesty International Report 2002, 2003, 2004* and *2005*, entries on South Africa; Amnesty International and Human Rights Watch, *South Africa: Submission to the Parliamentary Portfolio Committee on Justice and Constitutional Development, on the draft Criminal Law (Sexual Offences) Amendment Bill, 2003* (AI Index: AFR 53/006/2003); Amnesty International, *Stop violence against women: Violence fuels the HIV/AIDS pandemic in Swaziland* (AI Index: AFR 55/001/2004).

107 *Government of the Republic of South Africa and Others v Irene Grootboom and Others*, Case CCT 11/00, para 41, www.concourt.gov.za/files/grootboom1/grootboom1.pdf

108 Liebenberg, Sandra, "Basic Rights Claims: how responsive is 'reasonableness review'", Economic and Social Rights Review, Volume 5, No. 5, December 2004, http://www.communitylawcentre.org.za/ser/esr2004/2004dec_claims.php#claims

109 *Government of the Republic of South Africa and Others v Irene Grootboom and Others*, Case CCT 11/00, www.concourt.gov.za/files/grootboom1/grootboom1.pdf

110 For example, such concerns arose in the context of the response to the Indian Ocean tsunami. For an overview of human rights concerns in Nanggroe Aceh Darussalam (NAD) following the tsunami, see Amnesty International, *Indonesia: the role of human rights in the wake of the earthquake and tsunami* (AI Index: ASA 21/002/2005). For information on Sri Lanka, see web.amnesty.org/pages/tsunami2-eng

111 See, for example, General Comments 5 (1981) and 29 (2001) of the Human Rights Committee interpreting the derogation clause in Article 4 of the ICCPR.

112 African Commission on Human and Peoples' Rights, Communication No. 105/93, *Media Rights Agenda & Constitutional Rights Project v Nigeria*, 12th Activity Report 1999/2000, p. 64.

113 See, for example, Committee on Economic, Social and Cultural Rights, General Comment 14, *The right to health*, UN Doc. E/C.12/2000/4, para 45.

114 Article 54(1), Protocol Additional to the Geneva Conventions of 1949 (Protocol 1, applicable in international armed conflicts, although many of its provisions are reflective of customary international law, and are thus applicable to all states in all circumstances, with the exception of "conscientious objectors").

115 Article 54(2), Protocol Additional to the Geneva Conventions of 1949.

116 Article 17, Geneva Convention relative to the Protection of Civilian Persons in Time of War (Fourth Geneva Convention) (applicable in international armed conflict, and contains many provisions on the duties of an occupying power).

117 Article 56, Fourth Geneva Convention.

118 From Amnesty International, *Israel and the Occupied Territories: Under the Rubble – house demolition and destruction of land and property* (AI Index: MDE 15/033/2004).

119 Committee on Economic, Social and Cultural Rights, General Comment 3, *The nature of states parties' obligations*, UN Doc. E/1991/23, para 11.

120 Committee on Economic, Social and Cultural Rights, General Comment 3, *The nature of states parties' obligations*, UN Doc. E/1991/23, para 12.

121 African Commission on Human and Peoples' Rights, *Purohit & Moore v The Gambia*, Communication No. 241/2000, 33rd Ordinary Session (15-29 May 2003).

122 *TAC v Ministers of Health*, 2002 (10) BCLR 1033 (CC). For further information on this case, see chapter 7.

123 *People's Union for Civil Liberties v Union of India*, (2001) 5 SCALE 303.

124 Muralidhar, S., "Economic, Social and Cultural Rights: an Indian Response to the Justiciability Debate", in Ghai, Yash, and Cottrell, Jill (eds.), *Economic, Social and Cultural Rights in Practice*, Interights, London, 2004, pp. 29-31.

125 Robinson, Mary , "Advancing Economic, Social and Cultural Rights: the way forward", Human Rights Quarterly 26 (2004), p. 870.

126 When an occupying power exercises effective control, then the area under that control is considered within the jurisdiction of the occupying power. Human Rights Committee, General Comment 31, para 10.

127 Amnesty International, *Open letter condemning the abduction and killings of civilians and the "blockade" of Kathmandu by the Communist Party of Nepal (Maoist)* (AI Index: ASA 31/157/2004).

128 News release, *Serbia and Montenegro (Kosovo/Kosova): Protect the right to health and life* (AI Index: EUR 70/011/2005).

129 Maastricht Guidelines on Violations of Economic, Social and Cultural Rights, UN Doc. E/C.12/2000/13, para 18. The concept of due diligence is articulated in the decision of the Inter-American Court of Human Rights in the *Case Velázquez Rodríguez*, Judgment of 29 July 1988, Series C, No. 4, as well as in subsequent international instruments, such as the UN Declaration on the Elimination of Violence against Women.

130 Cassels, Jamie, "Outlaws: Multinational Corporations and Catastrophic Law", Cumberland Law Review, 31, 311, 2000/2001.

131 See Amnesty International, *The UN Human Rights Norms for Business: Towards Legal Accountability* (AI Index: IOR 42/001/2004).

132 Skogly, S., *The Human Rights Obligations of the World Bank and the International Monetary Fund*, Cavendish, London, 2001.

133 Maastricht Guidelines on Violations of Economic, Social and Cultural Rights, UN Doc. E/C.12/2000/13.

134 During the 1980s the World Bank supported the "judicious use of modest fees" in primary education. World Bank, *Education in Sub-Saharan Africa: policies for adjustment, revitalisation and expansion*, 1988, p. 55. It welcomed revenue raised from those fees into the 1990s: World Bank, *Primary Education*, 1990, pp. 44-45.

135 The impact of this policy on Zimbabwe was analysed by the Bank's own Operations Evaluation Department: *Structural Adjustment and Zimbabwe's Poor*, http://wbln0018.worldbank.org/oed/oeddoclib.nsf/0/15a937f6b215a053852567f5005d8 b06?OpenDocument

136 World Bank, *User Fees in Primary Education*, July 2004, http://www1.worldbank.org/education/pdf/EFAcase_userfees.pdf

137 Article 28 (1)(a), CRC; 13(2)(a), ICESCR; 26 (1), UDHR.

138 Annual report of the Special Rapporteur on the right to health, UN Doc. E/CN.4/2003/58.

139 OHCHR Draft Guidelines on a Human Rights Approach to Poverty Reduction Strategies, http://www.ohchr.org/english/issues/poverty/guidelines.htm

140 In association with the François-Xavier Bagnoud Center for Health and Human Rights, of Harvard University, USA.

141 *Saudatu Sumila v Attorney General and Ministry of Health*, cited at www.lrc-ghana.org

142 This was reportedly supplemented some years later with a complaint to the World Bank's Inspection Panel, www.lrc-ghana.org

143 From COHRE, *Online Newsletter*, No. 5, November 2001.

144 Legal Resource Centre, Ghana, http://www.lrc-ghana.org/what/health.asp

145 UN Declaration on the Elimination of Violence against Women, preambular paragraph.

146 Article 2(2), ICERD, "when circumstances so warrant"; Article 4, CEDAW.

147 Human Rights Committee, General Comment 18, *Non-discrimination*, 10 November 1989.

148 Report of the CRC on its fourth session, UN Doc. CRC/C/20, 25 October 1993.

149 There is an emerging consensus in international law that a child is anyone under the age of 18. Article 1 of the CRC, however, defines children as "every human being below the age of eighteen years unless, under the law applicable to the child, majority is attained earlier."

150 Article 32, CRC.

151 Opening Comments of Marta Santos Pais to the UN Committee on the Rights of the Child, Day of Discussion on "Economic Exploitation of Children", UN Doc. CRC/C/20, 25 October 1993.

152 Included in interview with Nathalie Prouvez, COHRE, *Litigating ESCR: achievements, challenges and strategies*, 2004, p. 140.

153 Article 7(1).

154 European Committee of Social Rights, *Complaint No. 1/1998, From the International Commission of Jurists Against Portugal*, http://www.gddc.pt/direitos-humanos/portugal-dh/relatorios-ce/cds6.html

155 Interview with Nathalie Prouvez, COHRE, *Litigating ESCR: achievements, challenges and strategies*, 2004, p. 140.

156 This may be temporarily set at 14 according to economic exigencies, ILO Convention 138.

157 Article 27(3).

158 UNIFEM, *Progress of the World's Women*, New York, 2000, p. 92.

159 CEDAW, Article 2.

160 See the "Montréal Principles on Women's Economic, Social and Cultural Rights" developed by a wide range of civil society and academic activists, available at Center for Economic and Social Rights, http://cesr.org/node/view/697

161 *The right to education*, UN Doc. E/CN.4/2004/45, para 34.

162 Martinez Cobo, José R., *Study of the Problem of Discrimination against Indigenous Populations*, UN Doc. E/CN.4/Sub.2/1986/7.

163 See for example, UN Committee on the Elimination of Racial Discrimination, General Recommendation XXIII (51) *Concerning indigenous peoples*, UN Doc. A/52/18, annex V, 1997; and *Case of the Mayagna (Sumo) Community of Awas Tingni v Nicaragua*, Inter-American Court of Human Rights, 31 August 2002, Series C, No. 79.

164 Article 30 of the CRC expands protection of cultural rights of persons belonging to minorities, provided under Article 27 of the ICCPR, to include children as members of an indigenous people.

165 The right to self-determination, Article 1 of both the ICCPR and ICESCR; and Grand Council of the Crees et al, *Assessing the International Decade: Urgent need to renew mandate and improve the UN standard-setting process on indigenous peoples' human rights*, Submission to the OHCHR, March 2004.

166 Recently recognized by the UN Committee on the Elimination of Racial Discrimination, General Recommendation XXIII (51) *Concerning indigenous peoples*, UN Doc. A/52/18, annex V, 1997.

167 Amnesty International, *Brazil: Safety and survival of indigenous peoples at risk* (AI Index: AMR 19/009/2005).

168 Amnesty International, *"Foreigners in our own country": Indigenous peoples in Brazil* (AI Index: AMR 19/002/2005).

169 Anaya, S. James, and Grossman, Claudio, "The Case of Awas Tingni v. Nicaragua: A New Step in the International Law of Indigenous Peoples", 19 Arizona Journal of International and Comparative Law. 1 (2002).

170 UN Doc. CCPR/C/38/D/167/1984.

171 UN Doc. CCPR/C/52/D/511/1992.

172 ILO, Towards a Fair Deal for Migrant Workers in the Global Economy, International Labour Conference, 92nd Session, p. 7.

173 UN Committee on the Elimination of Racial Discrimination , General Recommendation 30, *Discrimination against non-citizens*, UN Doc. CERD/C/64/Misc.11/rev.3, 2004.

174 International Convention on the Protection of the Rights of All Migrant Workers and Members of their Families, in force since 1 July 2003, currently ratified by 30 states.

175 *Thailand: the plight of Burmese migrant workers* (AI Index: ASA 39/001/2005).

176 See website of the UN High Commissioner for Refugees, www.unhcr.ch

177 See website of the Global IDP Project, www.idpproject.org

178 See Amnesty International, *Starved of Rights: Human Rights and the Food Crisis in the Democratic People's Republic of Korea (North Korea)* (AI Index: ASA 24/003/2004).

179 See UN Committee on the Elimination of Racial Discrimination, General Recommendation 30, *Discrimination against non-citizens*, UN Doc. CERD/C/64/Misc.11/rev.3, 2004.

180 Amnesty International, *Lebanon: Economic And Social Rights of Palestinian Refugees – Submission to the Committee on the Elimination of Racial Discrimination* (AI Index: MDE 18/017/2003).

181 Amnesty International, *Afghanistan: Out of sight, out of mind – The fate of the Afghan returnees* (AI Index: ASA 11/014/2003).

182 The Sphere Project has for instance developed a Humanitarian Charter and Minimum Standards in Disaster Response, which sets out the rights of people affected by disasters, and includes fundamental economic, social and cultural rights. See www.sphereproject.org

183 Amnesty International, *Sudan: Darfur: "Too many people killed for no reason"* (AI Index: AFR 54/008/2004), pp. 33-34.

184 UN Doc. E/CN.4/1998/53/Add.2, 11 February 1998.

185 See the exchange between the Executive Directors of Human Rights Watch and of Physicians for Human Rights: Roth, K., "Defending Economic, Social and Cultural Rights: Practical Issues Faced by an International Human Rights Organization", Human Rights Quarterly 26(1) (2004) 63; and Rubenstein, L. S., "How International Human Rights Organizations Can Advance Economic, Social and Cultural Rights: A Response to Kenneth Roth"; Roth, K., "Response to Leonard S. Rubenstein", and Rubenstein, L. S., "Response by Leonard S. Rubenstein", Human Rights Quarterly 26(4) (2004) 845, 875, 879.

186 Amnesty International, *Urgent Action: Mexico, fear for safety* (AI Index: AMR 41/029/2004).

187 www.tac.org.za

188 *Treatment Action Campaign et al v Minister of Health et al*, High Court, Transvaal Province Division, Case No. 21182/2001, http://www.tac.org.za/Documents/MTCTCourtCase/mtctjudgement.doc

189 Presentation of Fatima Hassan of the Treatment Action Campaign to Amnesty International, June 2004; Basu, Sanjay, "The Use Of Anti-trust Litigation For Public Health Advocacy: Lessons From The South African Competition Commission Case", December 2003, http://www.zmag.org/content/showarticle.cfm?ItemID=4773; Treatment Action Campaign, www.tac.org.za

190 See the recent series of manuals on the right to health, the right to food, labour rights and the right to water, published by the Human Rights Documentation Centre (HURIDOCS) and the American Academy for the Advancement of Science (AAAS), http://shr.aaas.org/escr.html. See also Law Society of Sri Lanka and the Center for Economic and Social Rights, *An Activists Manual on the ICESCR*, among others.

191 Article 19 (2), ICCPR; 13(1), CRC.

192 Reported in UNDP, *Human Development Report 2000*, Chapter 4: Rights empowering people in the fight against poverty, p 75.

193 Mander, Harsh, and Joshi, Abha, "The Movement for the Right to Information in India: People's Power for the Control of Corruption", http://www.humanrightsinitiative.org/programs/ai/rti/india/articles/The%20Movement%20for%20RTI%20in%20India.pdf

194 Roy, Aruna, and Dey, Nikhil, "Fighting for the Right to Know in India", http://www.freedominfo.org/case/mkss/mkss.htm

195 *Reliance Petrochemicals Limited v Proprietors of Indian Express Newspapers Bombay Pvt Ltd*, AIR 1989 SC 190.

196 www.freedominfo.org/case/mkss/mkss-lo.ppt

197 Robinson, Mary, "Advancing economic, social and cultural rights: the way forward", Human Rights Quarterly 26 (2004) 871.

198 Scott, Craig, and Macklen, Patrick, "Constitutional Ropes of Sand or Justiciable Guarantees? Social Rights in a New South African Constitution," 144 U. Pa. L. Rev. 1-148, 28-29 (1992).

199 The right to education is currently recognized in around 142 constitutions: www.right-to-education.org

200 The right to water is currently recognized in around 50 constitutions: www.cohre.org.

201 Fundar-Centro de Análisis e Investigación, International Budget Project and International Human Rights Internship Program, *Dignity Counts, a guide to using budgetary analysis to advance human rights*, 2004. http://www.internationalbudget.org/themes/ESC/

202 For more information, see Diokno, Maria Socorro I., "A rights-based approach towards budget analysis", 1999, http://www.iie.org/Website/CustomPages/ACFE8.pdf

203 International Human Rights Internship Program, *Ripple in Still Water: reflections by activists on local and national level work on economic, social and cultural rights*, University of Minnesota Human Rights Resource Center, 1997, www1.umn.edu/humanrts/edumat/IHRIP/ripple/toc.html

204 Summary included in Human Rights Internet, "Domestic Implementation of International Human Rights: litigating economic, social and cultural rights", www.hri.ca